HOW TO BE A

DEMONOLOGIST

G.P. HAGGART

© Copyright 2011, 2012, 2014 Greg P. Haggart

Cover art and written by Greg P. Haggart

Printed in the United States of America

Published by Create Space

ISBN: 978-1-105-36563-8

ISBN-13: 978-1478316398 (CreateSpace-Assigned)

ISBN-10: 147831639X

Third Edition

HOW TO BE A DEMONOLOGIST

G.P. HAGGART

HAGGART ENTERPRISES, LLC

"...THE DEMONIC SPIRIT IS A SPIRITUAL BEAST WITH THE WISDOM OF THE AGES AND THE POWER OF ANGELS."

ED WARREN

DEMONOLOGIST

CONTENTS

A WARNING TO THE READER

You may have bought this book for the whole purpose of the excitement of knowing how to be a demonologist. However, allow me to take this moment to inform you of the life of a demonologist.

Each day a true demonologist walks about his/her life knowing that someone is watching. They walk out to their car in the middle of the night and look in the shadows knowing full well that they are being watched. They sit in their home alone reading a book and hear a noise and wonder what may be watching from the unseen world. The demonologist knows that the demonic is always watching and waiting for them to backslide. The demonologist has religious relics and symbols on their walls to protect them. They pray everyday for wisdom and knowledge to better understand their enemy. The demonologist studies his enemy's every move, researching every step and action the demonic does.

Should you start to investigate demonic cases you will forever be in the cross hairs of demons. There is no backsliding once you are involved in demonology research. You will become a threat to the demonic world and their agenda, forever being a target. So take a moment before reading any further in this book. Put this book down and really think about what you are getting yourself into. Do you really want to live each day of your life knowing you are being watched? Or, do you truly want to use your knowledge to help people? If you truly want to help people then keep read on.

Here is some food for thought. The life of a demonologist has its sacrifices. He/She is willing to give of themselves to help their clients and sacrifice their time with their family while helping people on cases. At times a demonologist feels emotionally drained and some times can slip into depression.

Once you are a demonologist, you won't face the type of attacks that Hollywood might portray in the movies. Although parallelization, manifestations and other supernatural attacks do happen, the majority of the attacks that you will face will be on your mortgage, finances, health, family, friends, pets and authority figures that surround you, even the media might try and do one thing; destroy you by destroying your reputation. Oh no, the devil won't just try and kill you or steal your things, his goal for those who are a threat to his offenses against humanity is to destroy the saints by any means necessary. To be destroyed is to fall into a pit and feel as though you cannot get out; and *suffer*. The devil and his demons want to destroy you by ruining your reputation, cause your spouse to want to divorce you, take the kids, make you go to jail and cause a whole community to be against you. You will feel as though you amount to nothing when you feel a destructive path come your way. What ever you do to make things better doesn't seem to work. By then you find yourself wanting to get back at the world, and experiencing destructive thoughts.   Do you still want to be a demonologist?

This is not a game reader. The field of demonology is very serious having to battle against unseen beings that will stop at nothing to get at you. Many researchers consider the field of demonology to be the most dangerous field in the paranormal.

If you want to be a demonologist just out of thrill seeking, the devil has already beaten you. You were defeated upon turning the first page of this book or any book on demonology. You are dealing with a master fighter who is already in the ring waiting for you as you walk up. He already has the crowd of the *World* cheering in his favor and he can't wait to knock you out. He has already defeated you because you were curious and pay attention to what he does. He has already defeated you as a fan of demonology because you will stop investigating in the near future, you'll slip back into the world and be the subject of elusive attacks because you didn't close the door when you left.

ABOUT THIS BOOK

Hello my name is G.P. Haggart and I am an exorcist. I have encountered hauntings on every level all the way up to stage 5 known as the *dangerous stage*. I got into this field my last year of high school back in 1993 when I was attacked by a demonic entity. The attack against my life was so horrific that I have had to rely on eye witnesses to inform me of what went on. I suffered from possession and was alone in my battle against the demonic. There were no support groups out there to help me nor did any pastor have any knowledge on how to perform deliverance; needless to say I was on my own. However, Jesus Christ was with me the whole time and carried me through it all. Because of the attack on my life I know demons all too well and how they function. In some ways I am glad that possession my path in life to open me up to truth, and to provide a person like you with the much needed information on what its like on the inside. I could tell you stories that would give you nightmares. I've had personal encounters with angels; two have saved my life. I have also had conversations with demons during possession cases. I wrote this book because I believe there are many people out there in this world, like yourself, who could benefit humanity by being a demonologist. Like me, you've probably had an experience and obtained some invaluable information that can benefit humanity, save lives, heal the sick and cast out demons.

I know the main reason why you purchased this book is due to your own encounter with a demon. You want to research demons because you want answers. Well, coming from an exorcist's point of view I can tell you that all your answers have been right in front of you the whole time in the form of the ancient words of the Bible (2 Timothy 2:15; 3:16). That comes from experience. I just saved you a whole lot of mess and time by telling you that. Believe me when I say that I was in your shoes and I know what you are thinking. You are on your own journey to find the truth about these demonic entities. You got the hell scared out of you and you got a taste of another world you can escape too. You may even want some pay back by obtaining ancient knowledge, well because these things have to be ancient in order to put some hurt on them. You don't want to get too close but you want to find something that can act like a bomb with a timer on it, setting it off at the first sign of a demon. Well, my friend, as you study and research and have more encounters with demons you'll finally figure out that God's word is accurate. So I'll save you some time and money and tell you this; all the knowledge that you need to know on demons is in the Holy Bible (2 Timothy 3:16). Rather than purchase secular books on demons that will come from occult sources and only fuel the demonic, go to your local Christian book store and buy books from Christian authors who are in the field of deliverance ministry (1 Timothy 4:1-2). Each Christian author backs what they say with scripture so you can look at the scripture yourself and mediate on it (James 1:23-25). If you don't believe me then do this experiment during an EVP session in a demonic haunting. 1 John 4:1-3 tells us to put spirits on trial to find out if they are from God or not. If a spirit confesses that Jesus has *come in the flesh* then it is from God, however if a spirit *doesn't confess* this truth then it is not of God; put God's word to the test. So by all means get the spirit interested in answering questions during an EVP session, and then sneak in with the question. *"Did Jesus come in the flesh?"* Watch the spirit's reaction to this question. If the spirit is demonic it will do one of two things; stop all communication and maybe get a little angry, or it will say *No* and you'll be able to catch it in your recordings.

The Bible itself is full of knowledge on the subject of demons, however this book you are reading is designed with a curriculum of sorts to help you in your studies *to be* a demonologist. I will also show you the various ways to become a demonologist and get recognized as one. Each demonologist is not without their critics and every demonologist has his or her own ideas, theories and ways to go about investigating a claim. Much of the subject matter in this book is based on Christian demonology over other forms of theology. I'll also show you some important tools that will be invaluable in your arsenal to spot a demon. You'll learn some basics on occult/cult mind control, brain washing, mind control drugs, prescription drugs and my favorite, occult criminal profiling.

Figure 1 Photos of a 14 year old girl's room in Lansing, Michigan. She was practicing witchcraft and suffered demonic possession. The author performed an exorcism on the home along with two other ministers. The girl decided to go to church and vomited three times upon entering the sanctuary. Experts on the case believed she had three demons. Reports in the home by witnesses revealed objects levitating, manifestations, audible communication and shadowy figures.

WHAT IS A DEMONOLOGIST?

There seems to be a lot of confusion today over how to be a demonologist. Hundreds of people who study and research the paranormal have in some way encountered a demon. These people want to enter the study in order to use their experience to help others; this maybe you. Many of these people are real caring individuals who have gained some sort of special knowledge with insight into the strategies of the demonic world; however, many of these people are turned away as demonologists. Critics forget that their knowledge could be beneficial to the survival of humanity and to stop a demon in its tracks. Many people today believe that you have to be clergy to be an exorcist; this is not so. In fact Jesus specifically calls on *all Christians* to cast out demons (Luke 10:19). I know of many awesome non-clergy Christians who have a personal ministry of casting out demons and, these people are exorcists. The idea that you have to be clergy to be an exorcist is complete b.s., don't get brainwashed into thinking that only clergy can be exorcists when Jesus himself said in his own words to call Christians who follow him, "I give you power to tread upon serpents and scorpions and all the whiles of the enemy..." (Luke 10:19). The Devil loves it when man makes up his own doctrines to add to the word of God (John 8:44). This saves him time and effort to hold certain people back from experiencing a Christ filled ministry. To find what is true and what isn't is actually very simple. Doctrines that are created by either an angel or a man after what Christ and the apostles have taught are all cursed (Galatians 1:8). Your best bet is to stick with the teachings of the Bible and to find a Bible based church to attend.

Well I am here to tell you that you are a very important person in the battle against the demonic. Your interest in demonology and willingness to help those who are in desperate need shows that you are willing to walk up to Satan and at least slap him in the face. You may not win every battle and solve every case but at least you will show the devil that you are willing to take a stand. Don't mind those people who tell you, *"You don't have what it takes."* I know you've been drilled so many times by people with the question like, *"How are you a demonologist?"* The reason why you are getting asked this question is due to the fact that the demonology field is filled with dangers, exorcisms, talking to demons and supernatural events. There is a lot of knowledge involved in being a demonologist that can be very insulting to people in the paranormal community. Most consider the demonology field to be very noble and for someone new to enter it and start making claims can be insulting to those who have been involve longer. However, you had an experience with something and you are seeking answers. Didn't you? It is because of that experience you had that makes you important to the preternatural community; a much different community.

So how does a person become a demonologist and be known as a real one, an expert, and an invaluable source of knowledge when it comes to demons, deliverance and angels?

As an exorcist who has to work with paranormal researchers and demonologists I can tell you how to begin your work in the field. A paranormal researcher doesn't always need to deal with an exorcist, however the demonologist does. The demonologist is the person a paranormal researcher goes to when a case becomes or is demonic in nature. Researchers seek out a demonologist for one purpose and one purpose only; to help gain evidence that will convince the church to sanction a sacerdotal service. That's it. A demonologist is a person who studies the preternatural, which means supernatural. He/She not only studies the subject of demons alone, but studies other worldly beings that are supernatural. The demonologist deals with beings that are not natural with special abilities that could either cause harm or even death. More specifically, he studies beings of mythology and folklore that have connections to demonic functions that have entered our physical realm with one specific purpose; death. You could say that the main study of demonology is deathology, and it is the job of the demonologist to prevent death and destruction from taking a hold of a person or place. A demonologist is a wise researcher who understands demons very well to the point that his own actions can inadvertently help demons to fulfill their functions. This is why the Bible tells us that the Flesh is our enemy (Galatians 5:17-26). Should a demonologist or exorcist witness a victim of possession die during an exorcism, they have actually helped the demon fulfill its function. This is why you must be wise in all of your decisions that you make in cases and take the time to know your enemy.

The demonologist has a book of names and phone numbers of various exorcists in and out of his area. Demonologists have professional relationships with other demonologists and can get an exorcist over to a home quickly when something erupts.

The demonologist has a study in his home filled with books and a filing cabinet with folders of his clients' cases. He has a special journal of research to write things down when he discovers details about his enemy; which documents everything a demon does in a case so when he encounters a similar case he will know how to quickly solve it. The demonologist also keeps in mind to expect the unexpected on any case he works on, including the possibility of death. He knows that while on a demonic case anything can happen out of the ordinary, and he will never, ever underestimate a demon. Most importantly a demonologist is a preternatural detective to find the source of encroachment and find out how a demon entered a home of person.

WHO SHOULD NOT BE A DEMONOLOGIST

If you are the type of person who is looking to be a demonologist because it's the latest fad, or only plan on being one for a short time, then this field is not for you. Demonology is an investigators life's work, willing to give his time to help poor victimized souls of a demonic haunt. Once you start down the path of being a demonologist there is no turning back. It is equal to getting on a plane, the doors close and once the plane leaves the ground yo have no control to get back on the ground. You have just made yourself available to the Lord to use as a tool for deliverance ministry (Amos 7:14-15). Sure, you may take a break periodically in your life but the next thing you know you will be getting a call from a paranormal team with a demonic case while you are in the Bahamas.

If you have problems with addiction, pornography, alcoholism, abuse, abandonment, fear, the occult or are a thrill seeker then you should consider a different field in the paranormal (Romans 8:5).

Other people who should not be considered for demonology work are psychics and mediums (Isaiah 8:19, 20; 2 Corinthians 11:13-14). I say this because these are groups who are sensitive to the other side (Deuteronomy 18:9-12). Many exorcists will use people with the gift of discernment to help them determine if a haunt is demonic or not

(Romans 12:2; Matthew 16:21-23; 1 Corinthians 12:10 Acts 5:1-4; 1 John 4:1,6; 1 Corinthians 2:12-16). The problem here is that the demonic will notice who notices them. This means that a demon will take advantage of those who can sense or see them in order to gain control of them over time. If you are a psychic or medium it is best that you stay away from full-time demonology work so that demonic entities won't take advantage of you (Leviticus 20:27).

WHO MAKE THE BEST DEMONOLOGISTS

Those who make the best demonologists are the people who have overcome or survived demonic possession or a demonic haunting. Why? Because they have been dropped into the field by default and the providence of God will be revealed. Many of the demonologists I know have entered the field not out of curiosity; they enter the field because they had an experience. They are demonologists not for the fun of it, they are demonologists because they care and want to help people through something they have already experienced. They also have obtained a special gift by the Holy Spirit of discerning spirits (Acts 8:18-23; 10:30-35; 16:16-18).

The first encounter the demonologist faces drives them to want to know what happened to them. They will begin to conduct research on their own to find out how to prevent something from attacking them again. Ultimately, they find themselves getting connected to a case then their name begins to get out there among others in the field. Pastors begin to call on them to look into mysterious homes and individuals who seem to alter the natural aspects of physics. Suddenly the demonologist finds themselves engulfed in an unknown realm, meeting other people with similar experiences. They explore science and investigate cases on their own and finally discover that the only thing that can remove the problem of the demonic is religion.

The most common aspect I have found among demonologists is the fact that they each have the same drive in them. They are driven to seek revenge for humanity and to seek knowledge. The demonologist ultimately gives revenge to the Lord and allows God to work through him/her to help others who are facing similar experiences (Deuteronomy 32:35; Romans 12:19). These type of demonologists make good ones because they are driven to find a *solution* to the problem that demons pose. They do not seek fame or recognition, however it may happen out of respect and honor for what they do. Demonology is a noble field filled with people who have encountered nightmarish things that normal people read in stories. The field is noble because the demonologist is combating against a real evil that seeks death from their victims. Most people consider demonologists to be heroic for what they do. A demonologist willingly places themselves in danger to save a family. They are the gap that so many demons find frustrating that they will stop at nothing to put them away.

CURRICULUM OF THE DEMONOLOGIST

Demonology is not a playground; it is equal to two chess players moving their pieces to win the game. However, demons don't play chess they play a game of Go ("weiqi" in Chinese, igo" in Japanese, "baduk" in Korean) and occupy more territory with less forces. Believing that demons play war by playing by the rules, like the game of chess, is where many demonologists fail. You will be dealing with inhuman beings that play a game and in order to play the game you can't play it at all. The key is to not play chess but to play the game of Go. I'll explain this game later. These beings will try hard to get you to play their game, so you need strategy. Each demon is very cunning and skillful, and it takes a good detective to figure out who you are dealing with and why. A demonologist is actually very similar to a criminal profiler in some aspects, however in this field of pre-crime you are looking for weeds that are about to sprout. There are lives at stake and you do not have time to play games with an immature punk who wants to play. You are a super hero on the trail of a super villain and you got to stop him before it is too late.

What I find most interesting is the fact that demons are very much like serial killers. Murderers who like to play games with police to get them on the trail and set clues. The thing about demons is that they like to brag at times. Never take into consideration what a demon says to you if you happen to communicate with one. Always think outside the box and look behind the mirror. To do this you need to educate yourself on various subjects.

There is no real institute, university or college that offers classes on demonology. If you happen to find one check the school's accreditation. However, it is rare but many Christian seminaries and churches will offer classes associated to the study. In their curriculum there is spiritual warfare and deliverance. You'll find the study of demonology at a Bible college or seminary in the subject of theology and in part under the subject matter of *The Doctrine of the Father.* These studies can also be found at any Christian bookstore in the spiritual warfare section. Since the demonologist is a researcher that has one foot in preternatural research and the other in religion, the curriculum is very large; having to concentrate on all aspects of the supernatural. The demonologist's curriculum is not like the exorcist's form of study. The demonologist must know how to conduct research, investigate, interview, identify a demon and determine if a suggested possession by paranormal researchers is actually mental illness or truly something spiritual. Below I've outlined a curriculum of studies that are thought by many experienced demonologists to be a must in the demonology field. I've added a few studies to the curriculum due to the way times are changing and what I, as an exorcist, perceive a demonologist should know to help clergy.

If you find many of the studies below to be very interesting but you just can't afford the college tuition and fees to obtain the knowledge, there are various web sites that have college courses for free. You will not get credits for them but the great thing is that professors from MIT, Harvard, Princeton, Yale and 100 plus universities will post their lectures for free. Go to openculture.com, youtube.com/education, einztein.com and academicearth.org. You'll find that many of the studies in the curriculum below are on these web sites, or if you want extra math skills a great website is Khan Academy at khanacademy.org. The object here is that I know that you want to be a valuable demonologist and why not take advantage of these offers from 100 plus universities and touch up on your skills.

Diploma & Degree Mills

Let me try and solve this problem and allow for understanding on a very confusing subject. By definition a diploma or degree mill is an organization that is printing out diplomas, degrees and certificates on any educational subject for people at a price. There is usually a one time fee or a short range of course time to complete. They will take your money for a worthless degree that you cannot use in the work force. Many human resource departments of businesses will keep tabs on these mills so that if a person applies for a job they will know what institutions are accredited and what are not. However, ask any business owner about education and they will tell you that *experience is more important.* In the United States accreditation is not offered by the U.S. Department of Education. Let me say that again. *"In The United States accreditation is not offered by the U.S. Department of*

Education." Rather that the department of education *only* recognizes certain commissions who accredit colleges and universities. If the U.S. Department of Education only accredited institutes then it would be an act of socialism which is not acceptable in a society that practices capitalism. To allow the money to flow freely to stimulate education the government will only recognize those organizations that have set up commissions of accreditation. A government of a free society won't dictate how the people will be educated but will allow commissions to assign expensive tuition to colleges and universities to fill their pockets. These commissions have certain standards of education for colleges and universities to follow. However, institutions that offer college courses on *religion are not required* to be accredited because they are protected under the first amendment. This applies to Church studies, Bible schools, Bible colleges and seminaries who teach Bible teachings at a college level. Some of the most popular Bible Colleges and Seminaries will only get accredited in case their students want to transfer their credits to what Christians call a "secular college". So let me rephrase, normal colleges and universities get accreditation, while Church education, Bible schools, Bible colleges and seminaries are not required to get accreditation due to freedom of religion under the first amendment. Many Bible schools start out usually being a part of a church to help their ministers to become familiar with scripture before they ordain them. Still to this day there are Bible schools popping up everywhere that are completely run by a local church under their charter. Over time a Bible school will get a good reputation for educating their ministers at the church, so other local churches will seek them out for further education. The Bible school gets incorporated and begins to allow more students to sign up for courses to become ministers; generally studies in ministry, divinity and theology. Over time the Bible school becomes a Bible college with a full faculty, courses, credits and class time. The school can even hire a doctor of psychology to come in and teach courses on psychology and that would be fine because there is a form of psychology called Pastoral Psychology or *Christian Psychology*. Christian Psychologists usually have CPsy.D (Doctor of Christian Psychology) at the end of their name for their degree rather than the traditional Psy.D (Doctor of Psychology). The Bible College could even go as far as to become a university or seminary if they wanted and place deans over certain schools or colleges within the institution. And the Bible school does not need to be accredited because it is protected under the first amendment of the United States. However, this is not so in some other countries. For example in some countries it is illegal to run a college institution and offer degrees without accreditation. The United States Department of Education allows the freedom for institutions to decide for themselves due to Americas freedom of fulfilling the American dream. The U.S. government knows that if you wanted to start a college, you should be able to because it is your dream. However, without accreditation your college will not be recognized by the U.S. Department of Education. If you wanted to form a Bible school, Bible College or a theological seminary then you can without any accreditation. This is where the problem with diploma and degree mills comes in. Let's say you want to start a college but you know that you will need to go through the hard task of getting an accreditation commission to come in and accredited it. So you don't want to go through the long task of waiting, phone calls and such. So what do you do? Have your small college offer classes in religious subject matter and claim to be a Bible college. Then open an accreditation commission yourself and accredit your college. The problem is your commission board is not recognized by the U.S. Department of Education. To get students you then must offer low cost tuition and since you are a Bible college as well (but you don't advertise it) you can offer quick and easy courses at high prices. Oh! And you can offer honorary doctorates also; for an even higher price. There you have it the anatomy of a diploma or degree mill. Most people believe that all educational institutions should be accredited. But do you see the problem with that? The church is protected under the first amendment and if the government decided to do this then all Bible college courses would need to go by secular government structures and regulations. The church is completely independent from the government and the church would not want their teachings from the Bible to be regulated by a secular source. Simply put the church and Congress would not allow such a measure to happen because of the American first amendment rights to *"freedom of religion."*

Now many accredited universities and colleges do offer classes online so an online class is actually not bad because you work at your own pace. The Distance Education and Training Commission (DETC) is an accreditor recognized by the U.S. Department of Education who accredits college level courses that are taken online. A good example of an accredited university that offers online classes is the famous University of Phoenix. You can also go to the Commission of Higher Education website at www.chea.org and do a search to find a school that is accredited. Although the site is good to use it doesn't do justice to small colleges who are accredited by their state's department of education as a private institution. An example is Colorado Theological Seminary. Even though they do not need to get accreditation because they are a seminary teaching Christian courses, the State of Colorado accredits them as a *private institution*; meaning that they are accredited.

So when seeking an affordable degree in any of the subjects below be careful of diploma and degree mills. Check for accreditation at the Council for Higher Education Accreditation database at *www.chea.org/search*, or at the U.S. Department of Education site at *www.ope.ed.gov/accreditation* and if they claim accreditation from a state department of education go to that states website and look for them.

One thing that I feel that needs to be addressed is the fact that there are also paranormal institutes with educational websites popping up also claiming accreditation. Pay a large fee, take the courses and earn a bachelors in metaphysics or paranormal investigation. Be careful of these institutions also.

Below is information from the Federal Trade Commission at http://www.ftc.gov/bcp/edu/pubs/consumer/alerts/alt149.pdf on diploma and degree mills. This information will help you to identify a degree mill.

- No Studies, No Exams — Get a Degree for Your Experience. Diploma mills grant degrees for "work or life experience" alone. Accredited colleges may give a few credits for specific experience pertinent to a degree program, but not an entire degree.

- No Attendance. Legitimate colleges or universities, including online schools, require substantial course work.

- Flat Fee. Many diploma mills charge on a per-degree basis. Legitimate colleges charge by the credit, course, or semester, not a flat fee for an entire degree.

- No Waiting. Operations that guarantee a degree in a few days, weeks, or even months aren't legitimate. If an ad promises that you can earn a degree very quickly, it's probably a diploma mill.

- *Click Here To Order Now!* Some diploma mills push themselves through aggressive sales tactics. Accredited colleges don't use spam or high-pressure telemarketing to market themselves. Some diploma mills also advertise in newspapers, magazines, and on the Web.

- Advertising through spam or pop-ups. If the school caught your attention through an unsolicited email or pop-up ad, it may be a diploma mill. Legitimate institutions, including distance learning programs, won't advertise through spam or pop-ups.

In the end it pays to earn your education rather than getting your degree by a one time payment. If you are seeking to return to school for any of the subjects below, you can save from $350 to $500 or more and obtain credits by taking the AP, CLEP and DSST exams (www.collegeboard.org). These exams are accredited college credits and will be accepted at any college or university. Apply for scholarships on the many scholarship websites such as fastweb.com that searches for scholarships that suit you and always use loans for a last resort. About 15 million Americans go to college each year but only half of them actually succeed in graduating. Be wise, there are ways of obtaining free funds, getting free genuine credits, and getting through college quickly. The record for a college student who obtained a bachelors degree was six months. You can do anything when you think outside the box.

Chemistry

Those skills you obtained as a kid while playing with that chemistry set will finally come to good use. The knowledge of chemistry will help to identify potential problems in homes. An example of how you will need the knowledge of chemistry as a demonologist is to understand drug use. If a client is taking a prescription you should know the drug's interaction with body chemistry. Knowing how certain prescription drugs effect human behavior can help while on a case.

Knowing the various odors of certain chemicals can also help to protect your clients. While on a case in Howell, Michigan an elderly home owner believed that she was being plagued by demons. Upon entering the home my team and I noticed an odd smell throughout the home. I identified the odor as a chemical; however, demons will release certain types of smells including chemical (*theory*). This odor had a smell pertaining to bleach-type exhaust. Rather than allowing the home owner to be led to believe that the strange odor was demonic I decided to find the source (*hypothesis*). After a sweep of the home I discovered that the garage was connected to the back door. The chemical smell was in fact coming from the garage (*study*). Newer vehicles actually have a bleach type exhaust and knowing this helped to relieve the client that the smell was not demonic (*correlational study*). I recalled the chemical odor as being automobile in origin because I pay attention to my surroundings.

Also be aware of household chemicals and what they can do to the human body and mind. Claims suggest that demons will tend to use house chemicals against their victims to either poison or torment them. While I was on a Mid-West case the client *claimed* that the demon was spraying air freshener at him where ever he went in the home. Imagine a levitating can of air freshener coming at you. The demon could have easily used a lighter to set the can a blaze and use it on it's victim. Why? Because air freshener cans (mostly commercial) contain propane which any grill master knows is highly flammable. Other demonology research suggests that demons have used chemicals to harm their victims

The object here on knowing chemistry will allow you to get into the sick and twisted mind of a demon. If you were a demon with an objective to steal, kill and destroy (John 10:10) wouldn't you want to know where all the flammable chemicals are in a home? What would you do with those chemicals? Most household chemicals react to various levels of temperature and demons have been known to change the temperature in homes. Oh, and let us not forget about garages and sheds which have stored chemicals such as paint, paint thinner, gasoline, motor oil, fertilizer and lawn chemicals. In homes be aware of anything that can poison your client, an example is rat poison; which actually contains Coumadin (Warfarin) that is used as a prescription drug to thin the blood of patients who have high cholesterol. The drug is mainly used to prevent blood clots. When rat poison gets into the human blood stream and a person receives a cut it may cause severe bleeding and can be life-threatening.

Do you know what Dimethyl Benzyl Ammonium Chlorides can do? How about this one, do you know what effects Hydrogen Peroxide can do to the human eye? Here is a quick and easy exercise to help you understand the dangers of a demonic haunting. Put this book down and take a tour of your household chemicals. Go to your kitchen, bathroom or garage and try and find the product with this combination of chemicals. *Alcohol denat, isobutene, dipropylene glycol, hydrofluocarbon, propane, fragrance, isopropyl myristate, zinc phenolsuffonate.* Once you find the product read the warning label and imagine what the sick and twisted mind of a demon could do with it. Now do you see how blind we humans can be in our own homes?

Psychology

It is important above all other studies to understand the need for psychology to be a demonologist. Without psychology you can seriously endanger a persons mind should you happen to encounter abnormal behavior. As an exorcist I need to know psychology to determine if a person has a kind of psychosis and needs psychotherapy. There is also the problem of dealing with Dissociative Identity Disorder (DID) which use to be called Multiple Personality Disorder (MPD). Such a disorder actually exists and can be very damaging to an individual should you become aggressive to what you think maybe a demon. Demons will also use personalities (Also known as alters) that have pain, by bringing them forward so you can traumatize them more causing more dissociation in their victims mind; therefore more demons can enter. On several exorcisms I recall stopping a session because I've noticed the demon go under and bring an alter forward. Exorcism can be so traumatizing to an individual that if it is not performed correctly the clients mind will dissociate to cope with the session. This is the problem most inexperienced exorcists have who think they are dealing with a demon but are actually dealing with a screaming alter that is in emotional bondage. The inexperienced exorcist will try to cast the demon out and in the process the mind splits again through trauma producing another alter allowing another demon to enter (Luke 11:26). This is a tactic that demons use to maneuver around their expulsion. It's equal to a knight holding up a shield. The shield takes much of the blast while the knight is fine.

Another thing you need to know is that the American Psychological Association (APA) produces guidelines that help state governments to properly license professionals who want to be licensed psychologists. In those guidelines the APA state that a person "cannot" call themselves a psychologist without 1. Have received a doctorate in the academic field, and 2. Become licensed by the state that they reside in. Although a person with a masters degree in psychology can be called a psychologist as long as they are working under a doctor's license. So if you have anyone on your team that isn't following the APA standards for psychologists and calling themself a psychologist, they are not one and that title needs to be removed from them promptly.

You will also need to know the difference between a *psychologist* and a *psychiatrist*. Many demonologists and investigators often get the two professions confused or use them interchangeably. However, both conduct research and both practice psychotherapy, the difference between the two is simple. A psychologist usually obtains a doctorate level degree (Ph.D or Psy.D) and applies for licensure in their state to be a *psychologist*. A *psychiatrist* on the other hand is a *physician* (M.D.) who attended medical school to study mental health in order to better prevent it. Another distinction is the fact that psychiatrists can prescribe medicine while a psychologist cannot. I have seen to often young demonologists complaining that a psychologist did not prescribe medicine for their clients. Let me be clear, psychologists do not prescribe medicine only psychiatrists will. If you would like to work with a psychologist on abnormal behavior, your best bet is to find a *clinical psychologist*.

Philosophy

Most cults usually begin with a philosophy, an idea or thought on life. This is where you will need to study philosophy to understand the mind of the cult leader. However, philosophy is not just limited to the occult or religious ideals; every person on the face of God's green earth has their own philosophy on life. The *Ph. D* at the end of a doctors names for example means *Doctor of Philosophy* but with a specific major in a certain field. Take a walk down a city street some time and talk to the first person who crosses your path. Ask that person what he or she thinks will happen to them when they die. If they are a Christian they will usually tell you Heaven, a Satanist will tell you Hell, and the only person who is not sure will be the atheist; who will tell you that he will be a tree (I've actually received that response before). As funny as that may sound it's true. Most atheists I've talked to while walking the streets of various cities told me some very odd philosophies on life. Some told me that they will become a tree in the next life, others will just lay in the ground in nothingness, and some will be reincarnated. Now if the Christian is sure on Heaven and the Satanist is sure on Hell then it actually takes more faith to be an atheist to trust in those kinds of philosophies they come up with. Understand the logic of this philosophy? Where there is philosophy there is usually a lot of logic and thought put into it. Philosophy is the personal mathematical problem over the solution of life, the existence for the human consciousness and the media on which to comprehend ones own existence in the world. What is most interesting about philosophy is that one or several philosophies can only be brought down by another philosophy. Psychologically speaking, a philosophy is neither good nor bad depending on which aspect of ones personality is pleased, the Id or the Superego (conscience). Chances are if the philosophy is built off ideas that satisfy a person's Id then it is a chaotic and selfish idea. You will notice as you study world religions that most of the major religions are built off philosophy that pleases the superego. This is morality coming into play to try and build a better society. I am a firm believer that Sigmund Fraud obtained his ideas for personality (the Id, Ego and Superego) from the Bible in the epistle of Galatians chapter five. Read it while keeping in mind that the Id is the Flesh and the Superego is the Spirit. However, where I disagree with Fraud is the conscience is not taught by the parents. Conscience is very much alive in a person at a very young age. If you take a child who has a very large Id complex and take his toy away from him, he will still know that what you did was wrong. Basically he will know that the theft you made against him was wrong and he'll want his toy back; which is a characteristic of the superego. The human mind knows even in the early stages of personality development that theft, murder, adultery, cursing and such is all wrong. This is evidence for the conscience in the early stages of personality growth. Ever hear a little girl cry when a bug or bird is killed? The child knows that the killing of innocent creatures is wrong. This black and white area is later interpreted by philosophy. Where a young boy may cry when a fawn is accidentally hit by a car, he may later grow up to understand that if he doesn't kill a deer during hunting season someone may get hit by the deer in their automobile. The superego justifies the killing of the deer when the animal is butchered for it's meat and the man provides food for his family. Therefore it is logical to slaughter an innocent animal whose species overpopulates a given area that causes automobile accidents and deaths. By the hunter killing the animal it saves a small child sitting in the back seat of a car. You may find it hard to believe but the animal that kills more people in the United States is not the grizzly bear, black bear, brown bear, cougar or poisonous snakes. The white tail deer accounts for more automobile deaths in animal/driver accidents in the United States than any other animal. Non-hunters also do not realize that male white tail deer will attack hunters when they feel threatened. We are use to seeing these types of deer running from danger but often we do not take the time to realize that they do have antlers and they do know how to use them; including their front hooves.

By now you are probably thinking, "Man he just went off the whole subject." No, I was just giving you an example of philosophy.

Anthropology

This may shock you but one of Christianities greatest preachers, Billy Graham's highest degree he earned was a bachelors of science in anthropology. Why do they call him Dr. Graham? Dr. Graham had been given over 20 honorary doctorate degrees and had refused nearly as many.

Anthropology is the study of humanity, which has it's origins in the humanities and social sciences. You, as a demonologist, need to know anthropology to understand us humans, populations, race and the social framework. There is also medical anthropology (medicine) that is vital to the survival of the victim you are helping. As an exorcist I only allow CPR certified assistants to get near my clients during an exorcism. We take every aspect of knowing our clients medical health. As a demonologist it is your responsibility to know your clients medical history. You should know if your client has angina or heart disease, diabetes or is taking prescriptions prescribed by a physician. Never, ever tell your clients to go off their medication or risk being the subject of a lawsuit. The client must make their own decision to go off any medications that are believed to be hindering their mental or physical health. The client should consult their medical professional over the decision to be taken off meds. But never, ever tell your client, "I think you should stop taking your medication." You can however, tell your client, "If you feel compelled to take yourself off prescription drugs then let us know and we will continue." Then walk away from the case. Now that is not to say that you have to have your client's prescription free. I have consulted and helped clients who were on prescription drugs during their exorcisms. What I am trying to say is that if you or other demonologists feel that a certain drug is evidently hindering your clients' deliverance from possession, and then proceed to tell your client they need to make a decision before going any further. In a case I handled in Saginaw, Michigan I had performed deliverance on a woman which I had also counseled her sister; who may have been the source of the haunting during her practices with witchcraft in the home. The woman informed me how her sister would speak in weird languages, have fits of rage and her eyes would turn black when she was off her meds. She also informed me how her sister's psychiatrist had prescribed her drugs to calm her. I agreed to meet with her the next time her sister was in town. When she had arrived in town we had set an appointment to start a counseling session. When I arrived I met a normal appearing woman who greeted me and the demonologist I was with at the door. When we sat down and started performing curse breaking nothing was happening. I first took the situation as the woman was not demonized, but I went back and looked over her questionnaire she filled out. I spotted several rights she had given away to Satan, several strongholds with the use of many occult practices and evidence from a paranormal team that there was a haunting in the home. I came to the conclusion that the prescription drugs she was taking where blocking her deliverance. Just as much as a person's *Will* can push away a demon so to can prescription drugs alter the mind that can suppress demonization. However, it should be noted that the demonization is still there but is only suppressed to the area of the unconscious mind. The demon is still able to perform mental illness on a suppressed level because what is only infected is the person's brain. As an exorcist I knew I wouldn't be able to get at the demon and interrogate it on how it got in. So I informed the woman that if she felt compelled by the Holy Spirit to get off the meds she was on to continue with deliverance to let me know. Then I left the home. Never did I request to the client that she *had* to get off the meds.

While interviewing your clients keep in mind one thing. You are not a medical professional so do not give medical advice whatsoever. Unless you are a physician who wants to be a demonologist (in turn have degrees in medicine and in theology) and have accepted the client as your own patient in your practice; then you can take the legal responsibilities and allow your liability insurance to take a hit.

A client's drawing that helped to find the type of demon that was haunting. Depiction is of an Ori demon from the Orient that followed the victim's step-father to the United States after his time in the Vietnam War. The case was discovered to be a generational curse.

Cryto-Zoology

There will be times when you will be dealing with a demon that appears to have some connection with local folklore. I have dealt with demons that are impish, goblinish, with troll-like appearances and even features as reptilian. EVP's, client's drawings and photographs can lead to understand a spirits nature to find their function. Knowing cryto-zoology can help to find a connection with folklore and legend. You will be surprised to discover how much legend and lore has a specific connection to demonic cases. Sometimes finding connections between a demon and a character of legend can help to find a possible weakness. An example of this is sleep paralysis which is possibly caused by the hormone *melatonin*. In high dosages melatonin has allowed people to sleep better and have more vivid dreams. Melatonin

42

is secreted by the pineal gland deep within the brain and is sometimes referred to as the *hormone of darkness* because it is released into the blood stream of mammals at dark hours. Melatonin appears to regulate circadian rhythms during the sleep process, and patients of sleep paralysis have claimed to be fully awake but their bodies are paralyzed. This usually happens after REM (Rapid Eye Movement) sleep or otherwise known as *paradoxical sleep* in which the sleeper begins to hallucinate while coming out of a *waking sleep*. The sleeper emerges from REM sleep before the muscle paralysis characteristics of the stage have subsided. The sleepers eyes are open but they have entered a *waking dream* and still experiencing the dream while waking up. Sleepers report seeing shadowy figures, ghosts, and even aliens (Clancy; 2005 McNally, 2003). However, this psychological study does not help to explain the *spiritual aspects* behind sleep paralysis. A study done by David J. Hufford, Ph.D discovered a similarity that people suffering from sleep paralysis will witness a small creature come into their room and sit on their chest. Others with this disorder claimed to have seen a black mist hover over them. This condition is very similar to several cultures having record of these events. In New Foundland there is a legend called *The Old Hag* in which people will feel paralyzed while in bed and a small creature walks in and sits on their chest. Sleepers report that they can feel the pressure of the creature on their chest. See the spiritual connection?

When ever you run into a demonic case observe the actions of the demon as much as you can to find a connection with local folklore. Have clients draw what they see and connect the images to pictures of ancient creatures. By doing this you are more likely to discover a weakness. In the legend of The Old Hag, praying would cause the creature to leave. Psychologists who study sleep paralysis are now discovering that if their clients pray they are more likely to come out of the paralyzed state.

"Nightmare", 1800, by Nikolaj Abraham Abildgaard. Painting gives details and reference to sleep paralysis.

Occultology & Cultology

This subject should not be taken literally by the demonologist. What I mean is do not take the occult in as your own doctrine or theology. Don't ever teach the occult to people and say that it is factual. According to U.S. Census Bureau of the 85% of Americans who consider themselves to be Christians, 50% are Catholic with Protestants making up the rest. However, majority of these Americans according to the church are not true Christians (Matthew 13:3-9; Mark 4:3-9; 7:21; Luke 8: 4-8). A true Christian makes it a point to get involved in the church, family, God's word, has removed themselves from moral issues (including the occult) and gets involved in the community. A person who just calls himself a Christian but is still addicted to the lusts and negative influences in this world is not a true Christian (1 John 2:16,17).

So if you are an occultist who is a demonologist, my words to you are be careful who you help. You will be causing confusion among people who call themselves Christians (Jeremiah 13:10). What if after the episode they are having they decided to get into church? All of the pagan knowledge you filled their minds with does not coincide with Christian theology. The pastor or bishop of the church or parish would then have to reteach them proper Christian values. In the long run you may receive some backlash from the Christian community. The church is here to remove demonic doctrines not to teach them to the community (Acts 13:8-10).

For the demonologist it is a good idea to understand certain doctrines in the occult community but never practice them. Keep a look out for satanic covens and satanic churches because you will be helping people who have either escaped the coven or who have survived it. Learn about, but don't practice divination, witchcraft, sorcery, wizardry, psi power, necromancy and mediumism including white and black magic. Other forms of modern occult practices classified as "occult" by the church are reiki and yoga due to there connections to the new age movement and the practice of moving unknown energies. Knowing occultology and cultology can help you to be a source of information for a victim of demonization, and letting them know what they have done may have inadvertently invited a demon into their life.

Here are some more samples of occult practices: White & black magic, tarot or angel cards, Ouija board, spells, incantations, enchantments, astrology and horoscopes, sorcery, witchcraft, wizardry and necromancy. Other forms are doctrines such as, Freemasonry, Kabbalah, Wicca, Satanism, Spiritualism, Santeria, Voodoo, Theosophy, Rosicrusianism, Wicca, Anthroposophy, Reiki, Eckankar and Raelism.

The word *occult* comes from the Latin term *occultus* which means *to conceal* or *to hide*. Simply put the occult is anything done in secret for wicked and evil purposes either against God or attempted to be hidden from Him. False doctrine such as reiki or yoga can be considered to be occult because of the use of moving energy for healing purposes. This moves a Christian away from the Biblical practice of depending on the Holy Spirit for healing. No one is for certain where or what the energy actually is. Those who practice these teachings claim that it is their own energy that is being moved about. If you are a Christian practicing these energy doctrines please read these sobering words.

If you are Catholic the Catechism teaches that *"all practices of magic or sorcery, by which one attempts to tame occult powers, so as to place them at one's service and have a supernatural power over others – even if this were for the sake of restoring their health – are gravely contrary to the virtue of religion."* No. 2117

If you were to ask a reiki master where the energy comes from they would tell you that it is an "ancient mystery". In other words they are saying, "I don't know." Energy doctrines like reiki and yoga are considered to be a form of idolatry that breaks the first two commandments of God's divine Law (Exodus 20). This is due to the fact that these doctrines allow the practitioner to "center" *themselves* rather than allowing *God to be their center* in prayer. When ever a teacher of energy doctrines teaches you about how to move energy keep in mind that you are learning from a human being about spiritual energy and not something that is written in God's word. Always allow God to teach you about the things that are unseen and not man who only sees things in a physical plain (2 Timothy 3:16-17).

Evilology

Evilology is the study of evil. Evil's origin, purpose and function and how it got into this once perfect creation. Understanding evil will allow you to understand why there are demons and their purpose in fulfilling their functions. In a nutshell evil was invited into this world through the free will of Adam & Eve according to the Bible (Genesis 3:6). Though God has the knowledge of good and evil He chooses to do good things (Genesis 3:22). Many people blame God for their problems but the source of all our problems in this fallen creation comes from the root; which is Adam & Eve's choice to sin. God is a god of love, however there is no one more holy and righteous than He is (Exodus 3:14; Isaiah 43:15; 45:18). Therefore God must judge sin even though he does not want to (Ecclesiastes 12:14; 2 Corinthians 5:10). When ever God speaks it becomes a law upon which the course of the universe is sustained (2 Timothy 3:16-17). When these laws are broken by humanity it becomes sin (Exodus 20; Galatians 3:24). Sin itself is not evil; it is the act upon which it is performed (Romans 3:20). Evil itself cannot exist without good but good can exist on its own. In my book Mechanics of Demonology I talk about evil's origins and function. I explained that evil is like the rust on a perfect 1957 Chevy Bel-Air. The '57 Chevy rolls off the factory floor and the designers call it a great model. Once placed outside under a storm the car develops rust spots. Is the car now perfect? No, the car is no longer perfect because it now has imperfections of rust; which were not part of the designers original plans. The rust itself could not exist without the perfections of the car. You could say that absolute evil cannot exist without the perfections of righteousness. This formula can pretty much tell you how a demon gets into a home or person. The free will imperfections through sin can cause a demon to enter that which is considered by God a perfect creation.

Apologetics

This is mainly known as a Christian study, however if you are trying to lead your client to Christ to prepare them to meet an exorcist, it is a good idea to know how to defend the faith; especially when demons are tempting their victims to steer away from it. Many of history's popular atheists have become history's greatest Christian apologists. What is very interesting is a lot of the pastors I've met over the years use to be atheists; including myself. This happens when the atheist decides to read the Bible in order to use it as a tool against Christians. While the atheist reads the Bible and studies it he/she later discovers biblical truth.

Apologetics is designed for the student to learn methods to teach non-believers facts that are outlined in the Bible over the reality of everyday living connected to something divine. Where atheists preach about reason, apologetics presents the truth behind that which is reason that coming from the Bible.

Angelology

Many people who enter demonology don't realize that demonology is actually a branch of angelology. Demonology is the study of angelic beings who became evil and have fallen from grace (Revelation 12:7-10; 11:1-12; Luke 10:18-20). Many of my students find it easier to learn angelology first, to understand angels before moving onto demonology. However, there is a problem here. The occult has also begun to get its foot involved in angelology. Wiccans, New Agers and cults have taught their followers that we can speak with angels and have relationships with them. God strongly rejects the practice of the occult (Deuteronomy 18:10-12). There is also the issue of spirit guides that the very thought of which sends frustrating chills up my spine. The best area to learn about angels is in the Holy Bible, and how to do that is to go to your local Christian bookstore and obtain books from Christian authors. Don't be fooled into believing that we can have personal relationships with angels and spirit guides. Angels take order and seek only a relationship with God (Psalm 103:20; Luke 15:10; Hebrew 1:6). The very practice of speaking to angels invites the demonic to influence a person (Isaiah 8:19; Acts 16:16-19; 2 Corinthians 11:14). In interviews I have conducted and counseling sessions where demonization was involved, many of my clients had thought it was alright to try and develop a relationship with certain angels. They later could not believe that the loving angel or spirit guide who was helping them was actually scratching and abusing them.

You'll find that as you read from the Bible angels actually don't want to form a relationship with humans. They are more concerned with God than humanity. Their main focus is to take orders from God, live their purpose and be His messengers. Very rarely if ever will an angel appear to someone and when they do they usually say things like, "Do not be afraid" or "Fear not." (Genesis 21:17; Matthew 28:5; Luke 1:13, 30; 2:10) As an exorcist I invoke angels through the practice of deliverance but at no time do I ask the Archangel Michael how his day went. The angelic and clergy's main focus is on God and not each other. This should be your practice as well. The type of relationship that we exorcists have with angels is very similar to a nation's military ground forces requesting air support from the Air Force. The ground soldier does not have a personal relationship with the pilot of a fighter jet but they both have the same mission; to save souls for Christ.

Biology

There will be cases where mysterious objects show up and you need testing done. It is also important to study the surroundings on a case to get a feel of how plants and animals are being affected. Study molds, insects and animals which in fact demons can take control of; literal (possession) and non-literal (control and influence). An example of this is the demon Beelzebub who is considered *The Lord of the Flies*. In cases where this type of demon is involved witnesses claim that there are flies that infest a client's home. Jesus himself gives a reference to the similarities between insects and demons as scorpions.

I have also found in my research that insects and other types of animals, such as snakes in which Jesus compares to demons, do have eerie similarities. An example is the fact that demons will use their mouths to tempt a person knowing the words they speak are considered to be spiritual poison to our souls. A viper's (snake) poison is released through its mouth into the victim's blood stream. Some exorcists believe that when a demon enters a person they enter the blood. Other examples of animal and demonic similarities are unclean animals. In Matthew 8:31 and Mark 5:13 Jesus casts demons out of a man, whose demons ask for permission to possess pigs instead. The only connection that pigs and demons have is that they are both unclean. The Bible not only depicts demons with similarities as animals but similarities with plants as well. In the parable of the sower (Matthew 13:24-30) Jesus tells His disciples that those who are sinners in the church and do not keep the gospel in their heart are similar to *weeds* and will be rooted out. Though he does not say that demons are not weeds we know that demons can tempt humanity into doing things that are wicked. When we study weeds we find what any farmer will tell you is the fact that weeds can choke crops and steal nutrients that a farm plant needs.

Study and compare animals and plants to demons and you will come to understand certain demonic powers. You will also find that when certain weeds or animals infest a home that is demonic you will discover the type of demon that is involved; always pay attention to what is elusive.

Another reason why biology is very important to study in the demonology field is to grasp the fact that certain virus's will alter human behavior for the whole purpose of their own reproduction. Did you know that? Your body is actually used as a breeding ground for bacteria and virus's. An example is the rabies virus. The rabies virus will enter the human body and alter the behavioral patterns of the brain, reproduce and cause the victim to foam at the mouth so that the victim can bite someone else to let more viruses' move on and reproduce. Or another example is the cold virus. It was once thought that the reason why we sneezed was due to our bodies getting rid of bacteria and viruses. Actually the reason why you sneeze is the fact that again you are a playground for viruses to reproduce. The cold virus will alter a person's behavior to sneeze while it is in their brain. The virus enters the air where other people will breathe it in and the cycle starts over. This is how bacteria and viruses use your body to survive. Though the outcome for your body is harmful during these reproductions it is the way that microbes will survive.

By understanding this simple little fact on how bacteria and viruses alter human behavior to survive you'll be able to determine whether a person has symptoms of possession or is just plain ill from a bacterial or viral infection.

Theology

This is the study of God, plain and simple. There are several studies under theology such as Christology and Divinity that you need to know. Christology is the study of the life, death and resurrection of Jesus Christ and Divinity is the study of Jesus' divinity as God. Knowing Theology will help to combat demons, contend against them and know what tools and skills to use while on cases. An example is the use of the crucifix during blessings. Everyone on earth and in the spiritual realm knows that it is a symbol to invoke the power of Christ. Jesus spoke of the church as *the salt of the earth*. We all know that salt is a preservative. In blessings and ceremonies many churches use salt to represent this symbolism.

Understanding God will help you to develop a relationship with him and allow you to gain the knowledge needed to prepare for the battles ahead. The very best way to gain knowledge on theology is to get into a Bible based church and join a Bible study (2 Timothy 2:15; 3:16,17).

I consider Sun Tzu to be one of my mentors. His teachings in the Art of War have inspired me to apply his tactics to spiritual warfare.

The Art of War

In my early 20's I once dated a Chinese woman and learned a lot about China. Did you know that the Chinese language is one of the oldest in the world and has Biblical roots? Many of the Chinese characters in the language are in pictured form for a purpose. The character for God appears like three squares much like three persons. Why then three squares when God is one? Because the language is old and reveals hidden secrets of man's origins; God is a trinity and is why the character has three squares.

I fell in love with Chinese food and the culture. When my old girl friend and I fell in love she handed me two books, one on Chinese culture and the other was Sun Tzu's, The Art of War. I read the book cover to cover and learned Sun Tzu's tactics of warfare. Still to this day governments around the globe have their generals learn Sun Tzu's tactics of warfare. Businesses also apply Tzu's tactics to world trade.

The Art of War is so well defined by Sun Tzu that a person can decide the outcome of a war by simply knowing each military's might, character, heart, strengths, energy, power, tactics, spirit, weakness and most importantly how well the military force is disciplined.

An example of Sun Tzu's tactics is his methods of deception. Tzu said that without deception an army would not win. Because of this Tzu taught the importance of spies. In deception Sun Tzu says, *"When an enemy is far away make them think you are near by. When an enemy is near by make them think you are far away."* Another method Tzu teaches to gain more territory is by being close to your enemy. My favorite is that Tzu tells us that when we attack with an overwhelming force we must keep up the momentum or else risk losing the war. This is why so many demonologists and exorcists fail; they do not keep up the momentum when they know a demon is being beaten. After an exorcism a home must continually be pastured with blessings and the family be made to go to church. This spiritual method is equal to cleaning a place with spiritual; bleach; make the home white as snow.

When you learn the Art of War apply Tzu's tactics to spiritual warfare. Here is an example. When I work on two or more demonic cases at once and one is a possession, I find it easier to interrogate the possessed about the other cases saving detective time. This is similar to Tzu's strategy of using spies. Instead it is similar to capturing an enemy soldier and interrogating them about enemy plans and tactics (1

John 4:1). However, demons are known to lie but we can get around this with the help of the Holy Spirit who is the Spirit of Truth (John 14:17). By asking the Holy Spirit to punish a spirit for lying will get the spirit's attention that you mean business. The truth will come out of a demon when it can no longer endure the suffering the Holy Spirit puts upon it. However, the key to getting the Holy Spirit involved in a demonic interrogation is to take the possessed through The 10 Commandments. The possessed client's conscience will be placed back on the judicial bench of the mind and your client will be more likely to listen to the still small voice of God (1 Kings 19:12).

I previously mentioned to you about the game of Go. Allow me to explain a little more on this topic. In the game of Go you try to outwit your opponent by occupying more territory with less forces; therefore you must think strategically. Unlike the game of Chess, where it is frustratingly bad when you lose troops leading to your defeat, in the game of Go you may lose pieces but are able to still obtain more of a lead than your opponent. This was the way that Sun Tzu outlined The Art of War. We often think of war as a chess game but this head on strategy is meant for two equal powers. Notice how each player has the same pieces and each piece does a specific function. In the game of Go this is not the case. When Sun fought the neighboring kingdoms in Ancient China he did so without using head on strategy like chess. Sun won battles by guerrilla tactics using a smaller force. He would hit an enemy force larger than his at the weak points then run away.

When the opposing army was regrouping he would hit them again and leave making the enemy believe he moved onto another position when his army was actually nearby. You must adapt the same strategy when battling demons.

Think about it for a moment. The church has been battling demons for close to 2,000 years now. The amount that the church as a whole has been conducting exorcisms is uncountable. By this we can imagine that throughout history there are more demons than there are humans and according to the Book of Jubilees we can read that there is only a tenth of the amount of demons walking the earth; the rest are in hell. Strategically thinking we as human beings must obtain more spiritual territory over our enemy and the tactics of Sun Tzu prove that it can be done with what little force we are. To do this I recommend using the demons own tactics against themselves. If it likes to torment a family, torment it with Gospel music. If they like to tempt and entice a person, tempt the demons in a fashion that they come against each other; this is one of my favorite tactics in possession cases where there are more than one involved.

Demons have the ability to obtain information against us in mysterious fashions. They can strategically know about our movements and plans of attack ahead of time. A tactic I like to use in most cases where a demon is involved is Sun Tzu's tactic of attacking. You must always know when to attack the enemy. Most demonologists and exorcists will tend to attack when they are the strongest, but in actuality you must attack when you are the most weak and when the demon is at its strongest. Why? You will be able to observe its behavior while it attacks its victims, find weaknesses and later exploit them when you notice an opening. A demon may think he knows your movements (spying) but trust me, frustrate a demon enough and he'll reveal who he is by his own pride; this is another way to spy on your enemy. When I handle demonic cases I never rush over to a client's home, do a quick blessing then walk away. I like to know who I am dealing with, their weaknesses so that when the time to attack is ripe I can put some hurt on a demon. Allow me to show you an example.

In most demonic cases there are seasonal periods of rest. The demon will cause torment upon a family for specific times then suddenly stop as if it left. The theory is that they will absorb energy for long periods of time then when their energy runs low they rest. However, when Lent, Easter, Christmas or church observed holidays are right around the corner the demon will start up again. What I will do is allow a demonologist to be my eyes and ears on a case but never mention my name. However, if I plan to never set foot on a case because I believe a demonologist is able to handle it I will allow a demonologist to mention my name. This causes confusion among the enemy and is the same principle Sun Tzu's describes as I mentioned before, "When the enemy is close make them think you are far away, when your enemy is far away make them think you are close." Only during the seasonal hibernation periods will I attack my enemy when he is the most weak and vulnerable. Would you rather attack a bear while he is awake or when he is in a cave hibernating? I say go in and kick him while his guard is down. This way when a demon awakes to start another seasonal haunting he is caught off guard and notices the intensity of the blessing on the house and doesn't know where the blessed objects are to get rid of them. This tactic has proven successful in many of the cases I've handled. Remember, this is the *art of spiritual warfare* so always think outside the box, understand your enemy's behavior, weakness, strengths and tactics, then form a plan of attack and know when to attack.

Hypnosis

I know that this may seem to be an unusual study to have to be familiar with but the fact remains that we are dealing with beings that tempt and entice. Hypnosis is actually a way a demon can program a person to make them do things they don't want to do. Knowing hypnosis can help identify patterns in an individual to see if someone is being hypnotized. A demon will stay in the shadows and speak to a person's unconscious mind. An example of the unconscious mind is a person being asked to stop jingling their change in their pocket. The person may never have realized they were doing it until you brought it to their attention. The act of the person jingling their change was an unconscious act. There maybe a number of reasons how the change jingle got in their unconscious. Their may be an alter who likes money or at some point in their life they were poor and unconsciously they feel secure when they hear the sound of change jingling.

60

When a hypnotist hypnotizes a person they will usually place them in a trance and speak a function to their unconscious. Others that are close to the person will notice a change in the person who was hypnotized. This is usually done when the person receiving the suggestions are unknowingly playing them out. When I go on cases I usually stay in the background and watch everyone. I watch people and their body language and look for speaking patterns in everyone involved to find out if a person is actually saying things they don't realize. If I think someone said a subliminal message I'll stop everyone and look at the individual and ask, "Do you realize what you just said?" Most of the time they do not realize what they said, which causes me to watch them more closely. What I've noticed is that demons will use their technique of enticing to make their victims speak certain words without their knowledge. The unconscious mind always records events and speech that surrounds the life of the mind. This may also explain why demons will possess objects to be strategically placed in the background so that the unconscious mind will notice it. A person may have a fear of dolls because in their childhood a demon used a doll to reach their unconscious mind. In turn their unconscious mind picked up on that and every time the person sees a doll it acts as an anchor that unlocks the event in the unconscious mind. This happens without the knowledge of the person who has the fear of dolls.

Let's say you are having a conversation with a person and they are arguing with you over something. An example of subliminal hypnosis is strategically placed words within your sentence that the other person's unconscious mind picks up on. You want that person you are arguing with to do something, so you give them a subliminal suggestion. *"You have two choices. You can either **Say Yes** I want to do it, or **No** to do the right thing."* What happen here was the word *No* was made so it subliminally sounded like the word *Know.* The other person's unconscious mind received the suggestion and you get the outcome you want by them saying that they will either *think about it* or you receive a *Yes.* The *Say Yes* and *No* suggestions are usually said in authority with slight pauses so the unconscious mind picks them up. These are the type of patterns I look for while a possible possessed person speaks.

Direct hypnosis is when a person is placed in a trance when their conscious mind is preoccupied by starring at a particular object. A suggestion is agreed upon between the patient and the hypnotist. Suggestions may be short and to the point addressed directly to the unconscious mind. Below are examples of suggestions that a hypnotist may give a person.

For Drinking

You have made a decision to not drink alcohol. You will feel free of the desire to drink alcohol, and you will not drink it.

For Memory

Your mind will be like a soft, absorbent sponge and everything you concentrate on you will absorb like a sponge. When you want to remember what you have thought about, you will squeeze your mind like a sponge and you will remember everything you have concentrated on.

Neuro-Linguistic Programming (NLP)

Knowing NLP can help to identify lies which can be a valuable asset when interviewing a client and while interrogating a demon; interrogating should be left up to an exorcist. NLP is an advanced form of hypnosis and again will help to identify individuals who say and do things that influence others; including yourself. NLP is good to be aware of various signals that can cause influence and enticement. NLP also helps to train a person on rapport which is good to know in order to help your client feel comfortable with you. I make a point to always develop a good rapport with my clients so they can unconsciously feel comfortable with me. A person can sense a connection with you when you mimic their body language. The unconscious mind will pick up on the rapport while the conscious mind won't; only if the rapport is obvious will a client notice. Your client will feel comfortable with you over anyone else on your team. Building rapport is important because while the client may feel a connection with you they are more likely to take what you say into consideration. Too many times I've had to fight with my clients to take my advice to help them. I made it a point to learn rapport to have clients develop an unconscious connection with me. When you do the same you will find that it is much easier to talk with your clients. However, this is only one example of NLP. There is much more to learn of the study that can help you while on investigations.

Leadership Skills

When you receive phone calls from paranormal research teams to check into investigating a possible demonic haunting, you'll find yourself being expected to lead the investigation; simply because you are a demonologist. Most paranormal teams make it a point to only investigate and stay away from demonic activity. This is where you the demonologist comes in.

While on cases I've seen whole teams that are good friends leave a demonic haunting as bitter enemies. As the demonologist you have to keep the team together so this does not happen. Know full well that a demon will in fact try to divide and conquer. When it is able to divide a team the demon has more free ground to influence each individual.

A good book on leadership is *Dale Carnegie's How to make Friends and Influence People*. There are other authors who have written books on leadership such as John Maxwell. However, I find that the best materials to obtain are from *industrial/organizational psychologists*. Better known as *business psychologists* these professionals study human behavior within the stressful environments of business. After all running a paranormal team is like a business in all aspects.

The point here is to be the center of attention, which isn't really hard to do because demonology is a very curious field that not too many people experience. I usually teach leaders who have problems with their people in paranormal groups to always wear a different type of hat. This is similar to an Indian chief wearing a headdress to make him look bigger. The term for this is called *roostering* in which an individual makes himself stand out more than others to gain instant admiration. It is natural law that if a person wears something on their head that is special that they are naturally the leader. There are two reasons why I wear a black fedora as my trademark hat. The first is to mock demonic entities that appear to wear a top hat, and the other is to unconsciously take charge of the team no matter what team I help. Even though the leaders of a group are leading I am always the person who is looked upon by the rest of the group. I do this for one specific purpose. If something demonic shows up I do not want chaos to happen over who decides to take the lead. Leadership happens by default on whoever has something special or more than others, such as a person with a Ph.D over those with bachelor's degrees. Even though a person with a bachelor's degree is leading the team, they will always look to the person who is the doctor. In order for the person with the bachelors degree to gain leadership he/she would have to do something noble or rewarding to earn more respect as a leader over the person with the Ph.D. If he/she does not, then there would be chaos and argument over their position as the leader.

This roostering principle doesn't always happen with hats. A person can wear a special type of uniform, badge or even gloves. The idea here is that these special objects give off a feeling of confidence. Take a moment and watch your favorite television program. How much do you want to bet that each person who has gained fame from that program has something that stands out? A great example is the character of Abby Sciuto played by Pauley Perrette from NCIS. The character of Abby stands out in the show only because the character is a Goth chick and the actress has projected the character in the series very well. Should the character of Abby be killed off on the television series it would be one of the most watched and talked about episodes by fans.

Though these unconscious principles are good to gain power over others quickly, I stress the importance of learning leadership skills to keep your team together and everyone feeling important.

The story of St. George is used by many Creationists to support the connection that dinosaurs produced the legends of dragons. Many of the legends in dracontology actually resemble certain types of dinosaurs.

Dracontology

Originally a branch off of Cryto-Zoology, dracontology is the study of dragons. The dragon is the usual symbol that the Bible gives as an example of Satan. I have found that studying dragons from legends and lore brings a good perspective of demonic tactics and symbolism. This is one of my favorite subjects to study from as a hobby. What is important about this subject to be a demonologist is to study the lore from it. Various regions around the world have legends of dragons. These legends usually describe the presence of a dragon, its character and traits. Read the stories of the legends of dragons and you will be surprised to find similarities between demons and dragons.

Physics

It is wise to have a basic understanding of physics and the various laws that apply. This way when something goes flying across a room or something appears to teleport you can find either a logical explanation or declare it an unexplained event.

Knowing the laws of physics will help you on investigations to make sense of what is true poltergeist activity and what is not.

Metaphysics

In a nutshell, metaphysics is the opposite of physics. When something appears to be outside of the laws of physics it must be part of metaphysics.

Metaphysics is a branch of philosophy and deals with the thoughts on the world and of being. A person who studies metaphysics would be called a metaphysicist and attempts to clarify the notions on which there is understanding in the world. Metaphysics takes a long look at space, time, existence, being, objects, death and life outside of the natural laws of physics.

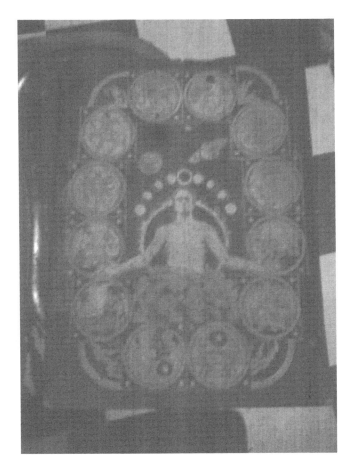

An astrological map was the source of a haunting. Map was discovered in client's attic.

Symbology

I find that studying symbols helps to gain insight on a case. Unexplained markings and signs with hidden meanings behind them can help at gaining more knowledge about a demon's origins and gain insight on occult practices used that conjured up the entity. In some cases I've handled I've found odd symbols had actually helped to find the kind of occult practice used that invoked a certain demon in a home or area.

Previous owners of a home who practiced pagan or satanic rituals may leave items behind when they move. I've found hidden symbols in attics, basements, outdoors on the property, closets and secret areas of homes.

Symbols on public buildings can help to identify principalities. This pentagram symbol on a town's government building indicates that the city was founded by followers who may have practiced either the occult or were of a secret society.

The basement of a Michigan sober house revealed old occult activities that were the source of the haunting.

World Religions

When becoming familiar with world cultures, world history and religions you'll come to understand how curses will operate and the various aspects and origins of occult practices.

You may even have clients of different faiths and it is best to be familiar with their religious practices to find the help that they need.

In a case I picked up from a paranormal investigator I had discovered that the demon plaguing the couple had attached itself to the woman's step-father while he was in Vietnam (See crypto-zoology picture). Her boyfriend has claimed to have seen the demon's face and described it to me. The descriptions match an Ori, an evil spirit only found in the Orient. His drawing helped to find the connection of a generational curse where the step-father took spiritual authority over his step-daughter; in turn allowing his demon to possess her.

So you can see how important it is to understand world religions to help your clients. Knowing the negative perspectives of world religions can help to identify evil spirits that clients have unknowingly encountered while in their travels.

Criminal Profiling (Criminology)

There may be a time where you will accidentally uncover a crime scene. If you have to head out into the woods or a field while investigating a case and uncover blood and bones you will need to inform the police. While conducting research on several cases I was contacted by a criminal profiler who asked me about occultology and demonic possession. I was about to enter the psychology field to begin studies in college. The profiler had informed me she noticed that each of the serial killers she interviewed were involved in the occult at some point in their lives. This doesn't mean that every person who plays with a Ouija board will become a serial killer. What it does mean is that a serial killer has a profile of being in the occult or was at one time involved in it. A profile is a model in which law enforcement follow that fit certain crimes.

You may find yourself hearing your client tell you how they had seen lights or hooded figures out in the woods, backyard or neighbors yard. I once received stories from a few clients in an apartment complex how they would view hooded figures walking about in the neighboring woods. If you happen to stumble upon a possible crime scene it is best not to disturb anything. Walk away and leave the way you came in, informing all members of your team to not touch anything. The typical occult crime scene is usually formed by satanic covens or devil worshippers; not the Church of Satan or Temple of Set. Most crimes involving Satanism are conducted by either people who are experimenting from small groups (covens) or people who have only a basic idea of what they are doing.

Expected items in satanic rituals are vestments, an altar, symbol of baphomet, candles, a bell, a chalice, elixir, a sword (if not a sword a sharp knife), phallus and a gong. These items are not all generally found at a crime scene. The most professional of occult criminal minds will do a thorough cleaning before leaving the area. You will find that those who get caught by the police are the ones who are usually entry level Satanists that want to go further with the practice.

Below are the types of rituals performed by Satanists. Each ritual is usually performed on Thursdays, Fridays and Saturdays. Witches will usually hold rituals on Thursdays. With each ritual there are colors, prayers, chants, words, meditation and sometimes drugs. The types of satanic masses are as follows:

The Invitation Mass: Usually offered to new members who are accepted into the group. Once the new convert has passed the rite of invitation he is sworn to secrecy.

The Gnostic Mass: This type of mass is generally used to entice people who are interested in joining. Demons are called upon to assisting in convincing the non-members to join.

Mass of Angels: During this ritual the powers of Lucifer are called upon to protect the High Priest from demonic forces. A cock is killed and the heart, eyes and tongue are cut out and used in a potion.

Mass of the Dead: This ritual is performed to remove the fear of hell from the celebrant while petitioning Lucifer. The mass also makes demons obey. A lamb is sacrificed having its throat cut. The lamb's heart, eyes and tongue are cut out, dried and ground into powder and buried with the lamb.

The Black Mass: This ritual is usually performed out of mockery of the Roman Catholic Mass. During the Black Mass men wear black cloaks while the women wear sexually erotic clothing. The priest usually performs this mass to recall a spirit, to gain power or to ask for insight into the future. The alter is usually facing the west and a nude female is used to help arouse sexual energy from the men. The nude woman is generally having their head facing the south and her feet to the north. All the men in the grotto have sexual intercourse with the woman and each member inserts a bread wafer into her vagina. The wafers are then ingested by the members.

The Satanic Crime Scene

In Satanic related murder cases there is less evidence at the scene than there is at self-style devil worshipper crimes. The inexperienced or thrill seeking individuals are usually messy in their attempts at devil worship. A true Satanist that goes all the way will usually be very thoughtful in cleaning after a ritual so that police will not have any evidence or leads. So pretty much, should you happen to fall upon a possible satanic ritual site you will be able to tell the professionalism of the occultists involved and how serious you'll be able to take the case. Satanic covens are more direct with their invoking and control of the spirits, whereas self-style groups will invoke and leave. Either way the scene should be taken seriously and any markings or symbols can tell you what was invoked and what type of ritual was performed.

At a satanic crime scene it is best to just leave things alone and call the police to come in and investigate the site. However, you are working a supernatural case so it is helpful to work closely with police to receive information. Once on site it is important to take photos from outside the crime scene and provide them to the police of anything that you find in or nearby. In any crime scene there can be contamination that takes place. If you walk through the crime scene or move something it can effect how police can conduct the investigation; and even harm any chance of police being able to capture the criminals. The best thing to do is to know how to identify a satanic ritualistic murder scene so you will be able to help police to know what they are looking at.

At a satanic crime scene there will be one or two circles of salt or possibly bowls of salt of different colors. Each color symbolizes something. *Black* for evil or darkness; *blue* for sadness, tears or pornography; *green* for vegetation or nature; *orange* for personal aura; *purple* for summoning spirits or spirits of destruction; *red* for blood, life or energy; *white* for purity or innocence; *yellow* for wealth, power, glory or perfection. Keep in mind that occult practices are generally made up by man and items used in rituals only alter the state of mind of the worshipper to better connect with spirits.

Candles play an important role in satanic worship. Though Wiccans use various colors in their rituals, Satanists on the other hand only use black and white colored candles. If there is candle residue left behind of different colors in a satanic crime scene then it can be assumed that the group is not organized and is centered around a cult leader; such as in the case of Charles Manson.

Criminal profilers have three different profiles for these types of occult crimes. *Type 1* is an organized church or coven. The organization is centered on most beliefs; however the core belief is in Satan. A *Type 2* profile goes by doctrine and organization including membership, rites and an infrastructure of leadership. The best examples of a *Type 3* profile are members from The Church of Satan and the Temple of Set; these are real Satan worshippers.

In the type 2 profile a coven is centered on a single leader. Type 2 groups are generally cults led by a leader with a specific agenda. These leaders will usually seek money, a mass following, do harm against the Church of Christ, or seek mass murder. If their agenda is stopped then the cult will either slow their progress or come to a halt altogether. Cults generally end when the cult leader is jailed or slandered. Never should a cult leader be martyred. Should they be martyred the cult will then become stronger and go into overdrive.

In the type 1 profile participants are usually self style devil worshippers, Satanists, cult members or live a Gothic lifestyle. A younger person is more apt to be a follower and participant in Satanism. The type 1 profile is more heavily involved in animal sacrifice, such as cats and dogs but have a limited knowledge of Satanism. This type of profile usually houses the suspect in a murder. The type 1 profile will usually try to please or act on their own in murder crimes. An example of this is *Richard Ramirez, the Night Stalker* who was a self-styled Satanist that acted on his own.

You will find that as you study material on criminal profiling it can be very rewarding. Just from reading the profiles above you have a pretty good idea of what types you may be dealing with when you enter a home with satanic connections. Should the adults inform you that they are occultists, they are more than likely either of profiles type 2 or 3. However, should parents tell you that their child is into the occult then they would be considered a type 1 profile. They should be watched informing the parents the profile behind their child. The fear alone of the profile type will cause parents to discipline their child.

Graphology

While investigating a demonic case in Alma, Michigan the resident informed me how the demon would communicate to her by writing on the bathroom mirror while it was fogy. The case was confirmed to be demonic by an independent preternatural researcher. The recordings, images, and video that he took confirmed that the case was in fact demonic. I agreed to perform a blessing on the home, however after the homeowner informed me of the writing I posed an interesting question to other researchers; *"What if graphology could be used to interpret demonic writing to help demonologists to understand the type of demon they are contending against?"* In some advanced demonic cases there are moments where a demon will actually write on walls, mirrors, floors and other objects to get their victims attention. Granted, much of what is written is very negative; however, I asked myself what if graphology could be used to help determine if the demonic entity were acting the part of a male or female. What if graphology could determine the demon's intentions and help to get into the demon's mind to anticipate their next move? For a century now graphology has been controversial due to its connections to pseudo-science, however, it seems the study has proven itself as an invaluable psychological tactic to understand human behavior in forensic psychology.

While on a case in Indiana I was shown photos of possible demonic writing where the suggested entity had wrote on the floor. The paranormal group that was with me was a very professional team. After looking over the photos I humorously asked if anyone could interpret the writing or had the knowledge of graphology. One gentleman from the team spoke up and said that he did. In disbelief I handed him the photographs and asked him to describe the behavior of the individual who did the writing. The others guaranteed me that their teammate knew graphology so I trusted what he informed me of. He described to me that the individual's behavior was of abnormal characteristics and the shape of the letters suggested the writer was female. That piece of knowledge helped in the case to ultimately understand what was happening.

The knowledge of graphology can also help to debunk any demonic claims. However, keep in mind that graphology will not help with messages that have been left behind on electronic devices. Each person's method of writing is very different and the structure of the letters made by the writer can be very revealing about the person's personality.

There is the possibility of discovering DID/MPD while reviewing writing in a demonic case, due to an alternative personality. This may be rare, however, keep this notion in mind should religious provocation not work to remove any scientific explanations in a case.

Something that I personally do to my questionnaire that clients fill out for me is a graphology test. One question simply asks the client to write out the sentence that is provided in the question. A few pages in the questionnaire there is another question with a sentence that talks about how great Jesus is that the client has to write. Many people don't understand why I do this but what I actually do is compare the two sentences to each other.

Not all the time but it does happen on occasion, the sentence referring to how great Jesus is has been slightly altered with different strokes which support the idea that someone else came through to write the sentence.

The best ways to learn the science of graphology is either to study under a mentor or obtain books on the subject.

THE PROBLEM WITH KNOWLEDGE

This may surprise you but the more you learn and gain knowledge to understand demons the less likely a demon will show itself to you. In the days when I was a demonologist demons rarely revealed themselves to me due to my intense first encounter. In my experience I have noticed that demons some how know how smart the demonologist is. A demon knows that if they do not show themselves to a cunning demonologist then no evidence can be obtained and ultimately the church will not be called upon. Some demonologists have had to sleep over at a home allowing the spirit to get use to them in order to experience what the homeowners are going through. I do not condone a sleep over because once the demon is comfortable with you; you are now a victim as much as the family is. The best thing to do should you start to notice that demons hardly come out when you are around in your investigations is to have paranormal teams investigate the case first. A paranormal team is more likely to gain preternatural evidence if they are experienced with demons. In a nutshell, let a paranormal team discover the evidence for a demonic haunting for you. This will save you time and energy to study other cases you are working on. If you obtain a case that is either in another state or near the border of your state of residence, request a team in those areas to investigate it for you before you can get to it. If the paranormal team finds no evidence then you just saved yourself a trip and a lot of money spent on travel and hotel costs.

Sometimes there will be cases that appear to have many witnesses and intense activity, such as a stage 4 or 5 haunting, which will need your personal attention. Many groups out there won't even touch a stage 4 or 5, and will most likely hand it off to a demonologist. With your extensive knowledge it is likely that your first visit will have limited activity. When you leave the family may experience a minor amount of activity due to your visit but by a week's time it will go back to where it was originally. You may find yourself visiting possible stage 4 & 5 cases three or four times until you start to experience something. However, the activity may very depending upon the strength of the demon(s) and their shyness upon your visits. Maybe the demon wants a good fight and it likes how much you know? It may even challenge your knowledge and want to cause you to doubt what you know.

In studying the 5 stages of a haunting, stage 3 is usually described as the typical haunt. However, as a demonologist you will be called upon more to research stage 4 and 5. To give you a run down of these two types of extreme stages I've listed them below with descriptions. These two types are generally hard for outsiders to believe due to their extreme measures. Due to the disbelief in these stages the demonologist generally has to spend a lot of time on the case to obtain proof.

Stage 4: Generally called *The Advanced Stage*. The stage has all the signs of a typical haunting but new manifestations are revealed. The haunting appears to be gaining momentum. The haunt becomes seasonal allowing the victims to experience the intensity of the haunting for a few months then the spirits seem dormant for a time. The cycle starts up again when either Satanic or Christian holidays come about.

- Flying/moving objects

- Objects disappearing and reappearing elsewhere

- Shaking furniture

- Pushing or shaking people

- Windows, mirrors or other household objects breaking for no reason

- Levitation

Stage 5: Titled *The Dangerous Stage* and for good reason. While the spirit still appears to go through dormant periods, the activity in the home now is in full manifestation. The spirit's object is violence and projects it's will upon it's victims. In these types of cases where dangerous activity is observed, most notably the spirit may have a goal to destroy the home by the use of elements such as electricity, fires, cold and other unusual methods.

- Biting, slapping or punching

- Animating objects

- Use of household electrical systems

- Hair pulled

- Heavy objects falling

- Sexual abuse

- Audible Voices

METAPHYSICAL LAWS

Much like the laws of physics there are also laws of metaphysics. Many paranormal groups and demonologists do not stop to learn these laws and understand them. By overlooking these laws you will make many mistakes.

Here are a few metaphysical laws that may apply to demonology. You'll find that these may sound like laws found in psychology, however many of these have been rejected by the medical and psychological communities.

The Law of Invitation

This law says that one person can invite another person using a type of reward to enter their life. A reward can usually be a gift, such as food, sex or something that the other person wants or needs. A person who invites another person into their life keeps the door open to that person until they close it. Generally speaking if you were to invite a stranger to dinner that person is now in your life until they are either told to leave, leave on their own or are ignored. The same principle can be applied to demonology. This Law works with both humans and animals; however the negative aspects of this law can be seen with animals more than with humans. Many people find that when they give food to a stray animal such as a dog or cat it is difficult to get rid of them. The animal now knows where to find food that it needs for survival. The door to the animal's invitation is closed when the homeowners either stop feeding the animal or takes it to a humane society. Generally we all know that if we stop feeding the animal it will move onto the next house in search of food. People who stalk others generally have been invited into the very depths of another person's personal and secret life. The psychological term is called *obsessive compulsive disorder* (OCD). People have found it difficult to remove a stalker from their life after they try to tell them to leave; which explains the negative aspects behind this law. A person who negatively closes the door on another person's invitation may find a negative response. The bear reacts with violence to the neglect of food from someone who gave it to them regularly. This is then called a *tease* which almost always has an outcome that is negative. When a subject is told to leave negatively they will respond negatively with harsh words and violence. When a subject is ignored negatively they will respond negatively in secret such as gossip, murmuring and covert responses. Depending on how a person closes the door to an invitation will determine the negative but opposite reaction they will receive from the other person.

In demonology the law applies the same way. When a demon is teased they can react violently. When a demon is invited in a person's secret life it will be difficult for that person to remove it. This is why so many women that are enslaved by incubi find it hard to remove the demon. Some women will actually enjoy having a secret sexual encounter with what they call a ghost. This leaves the door wide open for the incubus to have sex with a woman. Once a woman ends the sexual encounters the demon reacts violently.

Some people I've spoken with will use magick to close the invitation to a demon; however the end result is a negative reaction that many describe to me as "pouring gas on a fire." You will need a source of good to close an invitation to a demon, which is why the church always is called upon to help victims of demonization.

The Law of Attachment

The new thought law that "like attracts like" that positive and negative thinking brings about positive and negative results.

In demonology if a person who has anything in common with a demon and is in the same area as the demon they must have a demon. If a demon lusts and a person who is acting lustfully meet then the lustful person has a demon. This law can be physically seen by viewing friendships and how couples have behaviors in common to each others personalities.

In health science the law of attraction is very similar to the placebo effect. In the book *Love, Medicine and Miracles written by Bernie Siegal* it states that disease was related to a person's imagination, will and belief. He also wrote that love was a source of healing for an individual.

The Law of Control

This law simply states that when we are in high self-esteem and feel good about ourselves that we will feel that we are in control of our lives. The opposite of this law is the *Law of Accident*. The fact of the matter is that each of us is in complete control of our lives but when we have the sense of personal responsibility we fall victim to the Law of Accident.

The Law of Accident

This law states that when we have low self-esteem and feel badly about ourselves that we feel that circumstances in this world control us. When good things happen we benefit from life, however when bad things happen we fall prey and become a victim.

The Law of Cause and Effect

This law states that every action happens for a reason. This law is also called *The Iron Law of Human Destiny* because it is so powerful of a law stating that all actions happen for a specific purpose within human events. The Bible depicts this law in two different ways but very similar. In the Old Testament the law is described as "An eye for an eye and a tooth for a tooth" (Exodus 21:24), but in the New Testament Jesus extends the law by stating "Do onto others how you want to be treated" (Matthew 5:43, 44; Galatians 5:14). The Old Testament version is often misquoted as a revenge tactic; however it is far from it. In fact the Old Testament version and the quote from Jesus is one in the same. The scriptures describe how actions affect the circle of life of humanity. If a person performs an action of negativity then he is most likely to be treated negatively and the opposite also holds true. Should a person treat others how he wants to be treated in a more positive light, then chances are they will be treated in the same manner on which they acted.

However, this law also applies to events surrounding human existence. Because we have a just and holy God the wicked actions of humanity must be judge according to our sins. A great example of this law can be seen in the biblical story of Job when unforeseen circumstances be fall him.

In demonology this law is very important when confronting why demons haunt. The source of demonic power is none other than the divine law of God itself; The Ten Commandments (Exodus 20). When a divine law is broken by an individual a demon has the right through the law to perform certain functions (Job 1:11, 12). A demon's objective is death and the scriptures state that the soul that sins must die (Ezekiel 18:4; John 8:34). Therefore the specific function of demons to achieve the goal of death must be fulfilled. In the case of a demonic haunting the *cause* has been done by the victim and the *effect* is in motion by the demon to fulfill. This is why I've stated before that the study of demonology is actually deathology.

The logic behind this principle is the fact that in the book of Revelation when the messiah will rule upon the earth for a thousand years hell will be no more. The foreigner to God's creation which is death will not exist (Revelation 20:14). Man will no longer sin therefore the Law will not be needed. If there is no Law then there is no need for the demonic. However, there will be one last and final effort to get rid of the wicked found in Revelation 21:8. The sinners that are outlined in Revelation 21:8 are connected to Exodus 20 which reveals the 10 Commandments. These are demonic territories that these sinners have trespassed on and are considered non-believers and without Christ in God's eyes.

The Law of Belief

The law of belief states that what ever you believe with feeling and heart will become your reality. When what you believe changes your reality so to does your personality.

In demonology a positive force out weighs a negative force. The only thing that can remove a demon is a positive force. Your client's belief in a positive force is very important. Your client's belief will be projected upon the demonic in a positive fashion. For the Christian it is the belief that Jesus saves and can deliver us from evil (Matthew 6:9–13; Luke 11:2-4). This belief is then projected upon the evils that surrounds us and can remove them. In no way can a demonic entity be removed by scientific means but only through a positive belief in Jesus Christ who overcame the divine law can we find true salvation. In Paul's epistle of Ephesians 6:17, Paul describes the *helmet of salvation*. This is the *mind of Christ* that allows us to think like Jesus. The helmet is an important piece of the Armor of God in that it alters our state of mind.

The Law of Expectation

What ever a person expects with faith will become a self fulfilling prophecy (Matthew 21:22). If you expect good things to happen chances are they will happen in some shape or form. The same is true for negative aspects. If we anticipate that the negativity from a curse will happen then most likely we are allowing the curse to take effect.

Our expectations can play a key role in our outcomes on life, however we always need to put feet to our prayers (Acts 17:11). We can put our full attention into an expectation blotting out all other realities that our desires can make happen. If you expect that someone will pay you a visit in the next few days then chances are someone in some shape or form will visit you.

The Law of Correspondence

An old proverb states, *As within, so without* which is so true with this law. The law simply states that what ever is going on mentally in a person can be projected outward. Should you have to perform deliverance on a person always ask the person to think of their biggest emotional pain. A person's emotional pain is what a demon usually clings onto. By getting in touch with a person's pain can be projected forward by what ever personality is holding it. Usually the personality that is holding onto the pain is where the demon is usually hiding.

Internal pain can be projected forward onto our physical world. If a person is holding onto anger, he/she can project the anger forward in the form of hatred or murder; this is called a manifestation.

Surroundings can play a significant role in the outcome of human behavior. If a man has a dead-end job and can't find a new one or is turned down in interviews, the likelihood that he will project those feelings that were projected on him can magnify. The circumstances can magnify in the person's emotional status when something is at stake such as a family or a child.

While on a case in Clare, Michigan I had to act out the part as a marriage counselor while a demon was tormenting the family. Emotional feelings were being projected by the demon causing the husband and wife to fight. I asked them what was the cause of all their arguments and they truly had no clue. I asked them to try their best to *project* feelings of love, goodness, meekness, patience, kindness and joy in the home (Galatians 5:22-25). I did this to counteract the projections of hatred, lust, violence and rage that the demon was trying to make the couple do (Galatians 5:19-21).

Though highly debated among demonologists, red orbs are believed to be a sign of demonic activity.

ENCROACHMENT

This is a term in which you will need to be familiar with as a demonologist. Encroachment is the point in which the demon had entered a person's life. This takes some detective work in order to find when and how the demon entered. You will need to come up with your own detective methods to discover ways to determine encroachment.

To find encroachment one must understand the principles of divine law, metaphysical law, demonic rights and how demons function. As an exorcist I usually apply the divine law of the 10 Commandments and Old and New Testament Law, Biblical Rights that we can hand over to Satan (demonic rights) and the nine functions of demons. These are all outlined in the Holy Scriptures. To understand encroachment more get with a teacher or mentor on demonology.

SEXUAL ABUSE AND THE LAW

There will be times when you are on cases and discover a father or mother has molested a child. Should this happen do not hesitate to call the police. If you do not then you will find yourself in being arrested. When the police find you out for not reporting the abuse to Child Protective Services (CPS) you will be held responsible. If you are an ordained minister of the gospel of Jesus Christ it is important that you understand your rights. Many states have a law that is called the "clergy-penitent privilege". Read the following story to get a grip on this law.

In the state of Arizona there was a husband and wife pastors had discovered a father in their congregation who was sexually molesting his own daughter. These pastors decided between themselves to counsel the father in secret. The father repented and accepted counseling from the pastors, however after counseling he slipped back into sexually abusing his daughter. The pastors were unaware that the father had backslidden and the pastors neglected to inform the authorities. Years later when local authorities had arrested the father for sexual abuse, they had interviewed the children and discovered that the father was counseled by the pastor couple. This was enough to have these pastors arrested for failing to comply with Arizona Statute A.R.S. § 13-3620. Would the clergy-penitent privilege have worked in this case? No it wouldn't have due to child abuse. The pastors should have informed the authorities, however the pastors testimonies involving the father's confessions were protected under law so as long as either party kept their conversations confidential. As a pastor if someone confessed to you that they murdered a person, kept it confidential, a judge cannot hold you in contempt of court for not releasing information to the authorities. However, with abuse it is much more different.

Though you may feel an emotional connection with your clients upon discovering sexual abuse, do not hesitate to call the police over the matter or face jail time yourself. The Arizona story above is only one of many instances where sexual abuse was not reported by someone.

Though the pastors are considered to be in a profession it is wise to understand local, state and federal laws. This is also one reason why I ask a group in a local region of a possible demonic case to look into it for me before I take the time to investigate it myself. If the group were to discover something they would be more familiar with that county's laws than I would. It pays to be wise, not to be stupid.

The author looking over the basement of a building where a demon was present. *(Photo taken by Kathleen Tedsen of Haunted Travels of Michigan, Volume 2.)*

THE WORST ADVICE I EVER HEARD

One day I was surfing around youtube.com and found a paranormal investigator say in a video blog, *"I have said it before and I'll say it again, the church should not get involved in the paranormal."* This person also went on to describe how religion of any kind should not at all be involved in the paranormal. This seems to be a very heated debate in the paranormal community. However, as an exorcist this is the worst advice I have ever heard from a paranormal investigator.

Demonologist Tracy Bacon once said, *"Teams need to know where the paranormal ends and the preternatural begins."* The fact of the matter is you need to know the boundaries between paranormal research and preternatural research. In no way shape or form should religion be taken out of preternatural research. In the wise words of the late Demonologist Ed Warren, *"And I know that [Biblical beliefs] are fact because I've seen and I've heard and I've felt all the things that it talks about.* The thing is no one can afford not to have the church involved in the preternatural. The church has over 2,000 years of experience in the preternatural and has been directly linked to it. Many people argue that there are other religions that have been doing deliverance longer than the church has. People that usually say this are pagans but the fact remains that most clients who ask pagans for help in the end run to the church. Randy Ervin, a demonologist in northeastern Michigan and author of the book *The House on Church Street,* is an ex-wiccan (a Christian now) and practiced paganism when he was young. When he obtained demons through the use of magick he sought the help of a wiccan. Ervin informed me when they tried to use wicca to cast out the demons in his home he mentioned the same comment e-occultists say, it was *"like putting gasoline on a fire."* Needless to say occultists who attempt to cast out demons only appear to. Most of the cases I received in a single year of 2009 were due to pagan attempts to cast out demons.

In a case in Saginaw, Michigan where witchcraft was involved the owner had contacted a psychic/medium who used sigils to cast out the demons in the home. When I arrived I spotted how sigil symbols were written on ink-jet paper and duck taped on the couch and a couple of walls. I quickly removed them after discovering the sigils the psychic wrote actually conjured spirits rather than cast them out.

In a case in Taylor, Michigan activity got worse in a family home due to an inexperienced paranormal group's director having burnt sage in her attempt to remove the spirits. I describe in my book Mechanics of Demonology how sage can actually wake the dead and heighten the awareness of spirits to increase activity. Some groups I know use sage intentionally in known haunts to have spirit activity intensified for training purposes; please do not attempt this.

Though it may seem logical in some cases where occult knowledge would be needed, it is only a ploy by the demonic to make you and everyone involved practice their doctrines (1 Timothy 4:1). This way the doorway for more demons to enter widens. Don't ever fall to the temptation of using the occult to cast out demons.

The main teacher and mentor of a demonologist should be the guidance of the Holy Spirit. You can see how he works through people through confirmation.

TEACHERS AND MENTORS

Some of the best knowledge that you will ever obtain is from people who have mastered their own craft. I always suggest to a person who wants to be a demonologist to find a mentor. You need people near you who have been there, done that and have experience to bounce ideas off. Even in worse case scenarios where you cannot handle a case you need to get humble and allow someone with more experience to join you.

So the first thing you need to do when you want to be a demonologist is to find someone to mentor you. You can have more than one mentor to help guide you. Myself I have several mentors I went to and asked questions. Even still to this day I ask colleagues who have been involved in this type of work longer than I have for wisdom. Myself, I am a personal mentor to several people in the field. Not just a mentor in demonology but in deliverance ministry, theology, church and ministry planting and Christian psychology.

Another valuable source is teachers. Various groups and churches will offer teachings on demons. Attend lectures and seminars on the subject of demonology to gain insight from speakers who have theories, new knowledge or have been around longer than most people.

The important thing to note is that mentors want you involved when you say you want to learn. As a mentor myself I expect people to go on cases with me, handle books, tools and get things when I need them. I put students and apprentices to work while on cases. I figure if you want to learn the best way is to dive in.

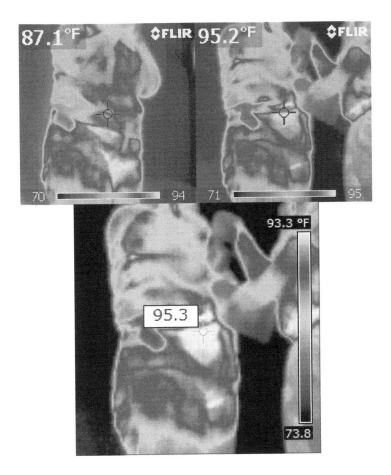

Thermo imaging cameras can help to support demonic activity. These images show the author performing exorcism on a client. Notice that the client is calm in the top images but when the Holy Bible is place in the client's abdomen the core temperature rises to white hot. *(Images were taken by the Mid Michigan Paranormal Investigators and from the book, Haunted Travels of Michigan, Volume 2)*

TOOLS

While in the field you'll need tools to protect yourself and even attack a demon if need be for defense. So below are some tools you'll need listed in two different categories. One is for research and the other is for defense or offense. A demonologist is both a researcher and a spiritual counselor so be prepared to work both the scientific and spiritual. Not only will you be gathering evidence for an exorcist, you will also be performing blessings when the need comes.

Research

In researching you'll need a digital or analog audio recorder, camera and a video camera. You'll need recorders to help in recording voices that the human ear can't pick up and imaging cameras to confirm visual sightings. The equipment is pretty much the standard paranormal equipment you would see most investigators use. However, I see more and more demonologists only taking a recorder, flashlight or a video camera with them. What is becoming increasingly popular among demonologists is thermo imaging cameras to pick up possible heat signatures formed by demonic entities that may have touched people or objects. In a case where I performed deliverance on a woman near the Flint, Michigan area, a paranormal team confirmed preternatural activity on the possessed by using a thermo camera. The victim's core body heat was normal until I placed a Bible in her abdomen. The thermo camera picked up white heat signatures, where she complained she felt something inhuman.

Some of the basic tools found in the preternatural field are no different than that of paranormal investigating. I myself like to use a KII meter; others use KII meters along side of trifield meters to confirm hits. I've seen these same demonologists use EMF detectors and a lot of funky looking gadgets to get a demon to do things to obtain evidence. However, one thing is vitally important to take on demonic cases is a first aid kit. You never know what may happen in the field. I've seen investigators scratched, hit, slapped and even paralyzed by something invisible.

In my own personal research I became curious of how demons are able to teleport objects from one place to another. Sometimes they will transport an object to another county and even bring objects in that are foreign to the home environment. So I looked into child locators to try and trick a demon into taking the locator, then using a GPS to find where the demon dropped it off. Use this in your own investigations. When a family claims objects are coming up missing, attach a child locator to an object in the home and claim that the object has some personal value to you. The demon will then be tempted to take the object just to torment you on a psychological level. On several occasions I have noticed that demons will take objects that have sentimental value to their victims.

Spiritual

Most churches will provide holy water to the public; however anointing oil can be obtained by your local Christian bookstore. On the other hand blessed salt can be difficult to find. You may have to ask your pastor to bless some salt for you. The type of salt I use for blessings is kosher salt. However, if your church commissions you as *"the person to look into demonic cases"*, then most likely you will be made a minister through them. I firmly believe that a demonologist should be a minister of the Gospel of Jesus Christ in order to better obtain these valuable spiritual tools quicker. Most exorcists like myself will provide holy water, anointing oil and blessed salt to all our demonologists.

You will need to use holy water to defend yourself incase of an attack. If I am pushed or touched I'll take my holy water out and splash it in the area I felt the force come from. "You get back from me demon in Jesus name!" Demons know when water is blessed and because of this I like to trick people to find out if a suggested possession is real or not. I've had clients drink water that was blessed without them knowing it. If there is a reaction then continue counseling, however if there isn't any reaction then pack up your gear and leave; don't waste your time. On a side note, should you obtain Catholic holy water becareful that you do not allow your client to drink it. Some parishes will mix blessed salt and holy water together.

Anointing oil can help in blessing a home and even in bringing a demon up out of the possessed. To bless a home you can take

106

anointing oil and place it in the form of the cross over doorways and windows while saying a prayer in the name of Jesus. Although, using holy water and anointing oil isn't a permanent blessing on a home (depends on the home owner's faith). What is permanent is using blessed salt for a blessing. Unlike holy water and anointing oil which are liquids and can evaporate, blessed salt is mineral and where ever it is placed it stays and the blessing doesn't ware off. I have actually had more success using blessed salt in the blessing of homes over holy water and anointing oil. Holy water should mainly be used for defense and for performing a binding on a home. Anointing oil can be used to bless a person and a home but for more permanent blessings on objects and homes use blessed salt.

Tools of an exorcist or an ekballist. This can vary depending on the type of activity. The basic tools of any exorcist is holy water, a Bible or book of prayers or rite, a cross, stole (visitation), anointing oil and blessed salt.

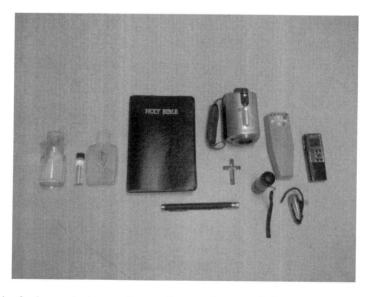

The tools of a demonologist can also vary but are always a mix between exorcist's tools and investigators tools. This reveals that a demonologist is both scientific and spiritual.

GETTING COMMISSIONED

Little do people know that most of the first demonologists actually worked for the Catholic Church. The Vatican would give a commission to individuals to be the specific person to go to when a family claims to have supernatural activity. Protestant churches will designate a person in the congregation to handle demonic claims or else the pastors would handle it themselves. If a pastor is interested in demonology research he may be called by both titles *demonologist/exorcist*. However, should a pastor only perform exorcisms he may sometimes call upon a lesser minister in the church to look into claims for him; this is usually a person who the exorcist trusts. Other times pastors will know a person who had a demonic experience in their past or who has an education in psychology. When someone comes to the pastor with a demonic claim the pastor will ask the lesser minister (who had experiences with demons) to find any truth in the claim. This lesser minister is in turn a demonologist.

The best way to be a legitimate demonologist is to get a commission from a church. Though they are rare it helps a great deal when faced by critics. Roughly a commission is where a church or legal entity will make a legal document under their charter stating that you are a demonologist and the person the church trusts to look into certain types of supernatural cases. With a commission a church will also allow a person to perform certain functions such as blessings and baptisms, which will benefit you when the need comes. The great thing about this is that the church will train you on how to perform a blessing and how to baptize people into Christ.

Any legal entity such as a corporation can commission a person for a specific purpose. It's not employment; however, the best way to explain it is in the history books where Christopher Columbus was commissioned by the queen of Spain to find a path to the Indies. Under his commission, Columbus had authority over the ships and men in order to fulfill his duties of finding a path. Corporations will commission people to perform special needs in the corporation's name. Under a commission both parties can cancel the arrangement at any time. If you are the director or founder of a paranormal team, and your team is incorporated, you can commission people as demonologists under your charter and it would be perfectly legal. All you would need to do is organize your board of directors together at a corporate meeting. As president, ask the board to give a commission to a certain individual to be a demonologist. The board votes on the commission and the secretary writes up the resolution to commission the individual as a demonologist. The voting should be recorded in the meeting's minutes for legal purposes. See below for a sample resolution for a commission.

ABC PARANORMAL, INC.

RESOLUTION, 0001

WHEREAS, the board of directors has determined it to be in the best interest of the above named Corporation to establish a department of demonology, be it:

RESOLVED, that John Doe is commissioned by the board of directors of ABC PARANORMAL, Inc. to investigate preternatural claims and is given the authority to perform blessings and preternatural research where needed. John Doe will be given the title of demonologist under this commission by ABC PARANORMAL, Inc.

The undersigned hereby certifies that he is the duly elected and qualified demonologist having taken the proper certification by this Corporation to perform such duties that are needed in accordance with state law and the bylaws of this above-named corporation on *month day, year* and that said resolution is now in full force and effect without modification or rescission.

IN WITNESS WHEREOF, WE have executed our names and signatures and affixed the corporate seal of the above-named corporation this *month day, year*.

_____   _____

John Doe II, President   John Doe III, Treasurer

_____   _____

John Doe IIII, Vice-President   John Doe IV, Secretary

A resolution is a statement of a decision by the board of directors of a corporation or legal entity. Resolutions are needed as legal documents so that banks, insurance agencies, lawyers and state and federal governments know that a specific decision was not just made by one individual but rather that a decision was made by the corporation (legal entity) as a whole.

A resolution is not like an agreement or contract; however your legal entity can form up an agreement or contract to designated persons as demonologists. The problem with a contract however, is that should you decide to use an outside source as a demonologist, the other demonologist that you have a contract with may take you to court for breach of contract.

With legal documents there needs to be an authority that is designated to cancel the agreement. This can be the president, board of directors, head of your demonology department or both parties can end the agreement at any time; but this must be stated in the contract. The best thing to do is to have the power given to both parties. This allows the demonologist you commission to cancel their commission should they decide not to perform such duties anymore.

HOW TO COMMISSION PEOPLE AS DEMONOLOGISTS

The governing body of your corporation, usually the board of directors, can get together and talk about who they want to commission. The board of directors is the governing body that makes all decisions for the corporation. Whether you are a Limited Liability Corporation (LLC) or a non-profit corporation or what have you. The governing body of the corporation can put in the minutes that they are commissioning a person as a demonologist and form a resolution with the corporate seal on it. No matter how much critics may murmur or complain about it the document is legal and binding and that person is a real demonologist.

In fact our church has commissioned ministers for the specific purpose to look into preternatural activity. These individuals are called upon when people ask our church for help. Our demonologists are the people that are asked to investigate demonic activity and find empirical evidence that supports the claim. These are trusted individuals asked to perform this type of work that our board of directors of the church has commissioned them for. They are licensed through our church charter and our corporation which is legal to the state and federal governments under section 501 (C)(3) of the Internal Revenue Code. Even if people in the public eye were to discredit them as false demonologists there is legal documentation that reveals them as genuine demonologists. This is similar to an accreditation organization accrediting a college.

If you plan to take your group down this path to getting incorporated, I would suggest that you have your own certification program to commission someone for the field of demonology. Invite someone to come in who has experience in demonic cases to teach demonology. Invite an exorcist to come in during a class to speak and answer questions. Once the course is over, have each person take a corporate approved exam. Make the exam tough and inform the students that if they do not pass then they will need to retake the course. The object here is to let others know in the paranormal community that you take demonology seriously. Once people pass the exam issue certificates that outline what they are *allowed* to do under the corporation's regulations. In our church's certificates to demonologists we only allow them to work in deliverance ministry, conduct scientific research, bless and perform baptisms. Should your demonologists perform other duties that are outside of what they are allowed to do then they should be punished. Write up policies and procedures that outline termination of their commission should they not follow protocol.

MENTORS APPROVAL

Another way to be a demonologist (some older and more experienced demonologists were formed this way) is to have your mentor make you one. Just as much as a Jedi knight would tell his padawan learner that he now is a Jedi knight, so to can a mentor with enough experience and knowledge pass down the lineage and keep the flame alive. He may either announce his decision to his colleagues or to the rest of his students. This method of becoming a demonologist is very noble coming from a person who has a wealth of experience. This is much like medieval knights knighting their squire to prepare them for war.

Great demonologists like John Zaffis, Tracy Bacon and Keith Johnson all had mentors they looked up to and gained knowledge from. One of the best mentors and respected individuals of the paranormal community is the late Ed Warren. Today there are several respected individuals who are demonologists who take apprentices and teach them all they know. This is one of the best ways to be a demonologist over any other method. Not only do you gain friendship from a respected person in the community of demonology, you also gain a wealth of knowledge that has been handed down from generation to generation. Also, should a group seek help from a well known demonologist and are unable to get in contact with them, you will be the next in line due to the fact that you were known to be mentored by them.

CALLING YOURSELF A DEMONOLOGIST

It frustrates me when critics of demonology slander people who call themselves a demonologist. My questions to these critics are: Are you a reliable source of demonology? If so then why aren't you a demonologist?

To be honest there really isn't any actual set in stone way to be a demonologist except for gaining a commission under a corporation's charter, or obtaining approval from a mentor or just calling yourself one. A demonologist can be described as a person who studies demons; that's it. So if you have a hobby of collecting demonic things, preternatural and occult material, or just like to study the subject of demons, then you *are* a demonologist. Some people have grown a reputation for being a demonologist not just for handling demonic cases but simply studying the field as a hobby. Friends, family and the town they live in understand their hobby, then one day a police officer knocks on their door asking for help to solve an occult related crime.

Though this way of becoming a demonologist is frowned upon by many in the paranormal community, studying demons without a mentor or a commission and calling yourself one is no different than being an amateur astronomer. Anyone can purchase a telescope and computer software and observe the rotation of the stars and planets. An amateur astronomer may be a hobbyist who enjoys star gazing merely for pleasure and not for the scientific aspect of it. A person who calls themself a demonologist without being mentored or commissioned is nothing more than a person who studies the demonic as a hobbyist. If you are serious about becoming a demonologist then get with a mentor or work with an organization that studies the preternatural. In a nutshell, a true demonologist is passionate about the field and wants to solve the demonic problem. Do you have this type of passion for the field? Or are you just in it for a little while then leave? 15 minutes of fame in demonology and satisfaction is not worth 15 minutes of demonic torment.

The author performing an exorcism on a woman with three devils. Demonologist Tracy Bacon on the left and prayer warrior James Allen on the right.

The author performing deliverance on a woman in a Northern Michigan home.

The author performing an exorcism, Book: Haunted Travels of Michigan, Volume 2 by Kathleen Tedsen and Beverly Rydel.

WHAT TO EXPECT IN THE FIELD

You have a demonic case and have evidence to prove it. You bring your case to an exorcist. The exorcist looks over your case and tells you that he will get back with you on a decision on how the church will proceed. Finally, the church calls you and has sanctioned an exorcism. O.k. it's now time for you to walk away and let the church handle the case. Um… nope it isn't. It's your case and you have to see it through. Even if half way through the process of exorcism the exorcist says he's going to stop and let the possessed go home, you need to be there for your client. Even if the church is suddenly done with the case, you need to be there for your client. The point is there really is no position on your part to truly walk away. You need to see the case through and assist your client at all cost. Once you take a case there is no turning back unless there is fraud. You're stuck and the devil knows it. If you walk away in the middle of a case you've left the client open to receive attacks from more demons.

My advice to you is never to have too much on your plate. What I mean by this is do not take on a bunch of cases that you know you cannot handle. Be humble and be willing to give cases over to other experienced demonologists. This way the people who come to you will get helped. Always work on one case at a time and give it your full attention until the end; always see it through. Even if you are in one state and you receive a case miles away in another state, give that case over to someone that is close by unless you have the funds to race over there and help out every time there is an attack. Keep in mind that spiritual health is similar to physical health. If someone has a heart attack you don't take them to a hospital in another state. No, you take them to the hospital that is close by unless their injuries call for a hospital that specializes in a specific medical field related to their injuries. When you get a case that is far away, give it to a researcher or paranormal team that specializes in demonology in that area. When there is an emergency, specialists nearby can better take care of the situation than you can.

Should you overwhelm yourself with cases you'll find yourself having a reputation of not following through. Your clients will tell others how you pick and choose your cases and ignore them. It is better to help new clients by seeking help for them in their area than be a case hogger and have them wait months for you to arrive.

MAPPING COVENS

When you become a demonologist one of the most important things to do is to document satanic coven locations. Most of the demonologists and exorcists that I know will try their best to keep tabs on these sinister groups. The reason behind keeping track of these groups is so important due to the fact that there is a link between demonic hauntings and satanic coven activity in given areas. You will find that as you investigate claims you'll begin to see the correlation in certain cities that you know have covens.

On one occasion demonologist Tracy Bacon had informed me how he was amazed that most of the cases he obtained were near state lines. He had asked me if I knew of a reason for this. At the time I wasn't sure but I kept a mental note. So I drew up a theory that satanic covens operate on state lines to avoid detection and that there was a connection to demonic hauntings. I called this theory, *Occult Operational Theory*. The following year I was working with another demonologist from Kentucky, on a case who had informed me how he knew of covens that stayed near the borders of his state to avoid detection. There were many more demonologists who reported the same activity near the borders of their states. This drew a connection between state line haunts and satanic coven operations; this is called a *positive correlation* in psychological research. Although this doesn't prove my hypothesis that satanic covens are on state borders to avoid detection and hauntings, it only reveals that there is a connection. So you can see how satanic worship by Satanists may have an effect on an area. It is best while on an investigation to find out where the nearest coven is, however keep in mind that Wicca and Satanism is not the same thing and do not confuse them as being the same. Each occult religion believes they worship something different than the other, however in the church's eye they are one in the same in their worship of a false deity.

In some cases where you will find a satanic coven worshipping near by, a simple blessing or a visit by an exorcist can make a difference. Demons may wander off from the Satanists ritual location and see what they can torment or enslave. By performing a blessing on the home you can cause the demon to leave and not return. This is not the case when you find the actual source that is causing the hauntings in the area. You may be discovering a principality of demons. At one time I kept receiving case after case from around the Alma, Michigan area but could never find the source of all the hauntings. In each client's home, during visitations that had a claim with evidence, the family would report from a few days to a week that there was no activity after I left.

INDIVIDUAL HAUNTS

Haunts that involve a single individual are much different than investigating cases where satanic covens are near by. Haunts that involve an individual find their sources in mistakes made by the client. I have always found that individual haunts usually always involve a spirit board of some kind. A person will usually want to know some kind of hidden knowledge so they either purchase or make a spirit board to summon a spirit to gain information. Other cases happen due to an individual having unresolved emotional issues and wandering off to a site where occult worship is occurring. They return home only to find something has attached itself to them. I find that these people become so curious that they cannot help but to touch some of the artifacts around the site.

In a case near the border of Indiana and Michigan a satanic coven was believed to be in the area and burning items for worship. As to what the items were could not be confirmed. A neighbor woman snooped over and touched what she claimed to be a human skull. However, she had claimed that when she went over to the area again the skull was gone. Since her visits to the worship site she and her daughters claimed to be experiencing strange activity. As a demonologist this is where the knowledge of psychology comes into play. John and Karen Mealer, the demonologists that researched the case found that the mother had been experiencing black outs and had what appeared to be schizophrenia. The mother had continued to claim that she was seeing people surrounding her home and starring in. Because of it she felt the need to purchase a shotgun and have it loaded at all times. She also slept with a bowie knife under her pillow in case someone broke in and entered her bedroom. These are the types of dangers that you would need to expect as a demonologist. John and Karen made a psychological determination, and had requested that the mother seek counseling from a professional before they would continue researching any demonic claims in her case. It is important to have any weapons removed from the home when you obtain such cases when the suspicion of mental illness is involved. In the case above demonologist John Mealer had discovered that the shotgun was loaded and the safety off. Unfortunately he discovered that the safety was off when the shotgun lost its footing and began falling to the floor. He had grabbed the gun just in time before it would hit the floor and discharge. Seeing the danger behind the situation he asked the mother to unload the gun and reveal any other weapons that she had stored in secret places. Now you see the dangers of dealing with abnormal psychology. If you are not experienced with psychotherapy do not try to be a hero.

You will find that in individual cases there is likely to be a possession or attachment of some kind. This is where your training and skills you obtained from mentors, teachers, books and lectures will be helpful. You will need to stay with your client and be available when they need help. Also, you will need to know if the home needs a blessing or if an individual needs deliverance. Is it a psychosis or is it

124

demonic possession? One false move and you could make matters worse.

TESTING TO SEE IF SOMEONE IS POSSESSED

Stronger demons will usually be all too willing to come out and confront you, however most usually hide for fear of confronting God. In some possession cases I have handled all I needed to do was command the demon to come forward to start the interrogation. In others I have had to explore Dissociative Identity Disorder/Multiple Personality Disorder (DID/MPD) to find the deepest pain to see where the demon was attached to what alternative personality. However, there are easier and simpler ways to have a demon come forward. You will need to see for yourself if someone is truly possessed in order to convince us exorcists that there is something supernatural going on.

One method is to hand a blessed cross to a partner. While you are talking to your client secretly signal your partner to walk behind the person and place the blessed cross six inches behind the client's neck. If they are possessed then the demon will confront you or you should see some signs of discomfort in your client. If nothing happens then it is possible that the client is not possessed. However, keep in mind higher level demons (powers, rulers of the darkness of this world, high places; Ephesians 6:12) are able to resist blessed objects.

Another method is when the client asks for a cup of water, walk into the kitchen and put some holy water in a cup rather than regular tap water. Once you walk up to your client the demons in them will either start to react to the cup in front of you, or when the client drinks it they may become sick to their stomach. As you can see demons will have a reaction of some kind to blessed objects. Even if you have a blessed cane and you touch your client with it demons will react to it. This method of using blessed objects without client knowledge (Although you should inform them before any investigation that you intend to) is a supernatural way to find the boundary between psychosis and possession. The point is the client doesn't know that the objects are blessed. With the client not knowing this allows for illusive communication with the demon(s) in the soul. If you are not familiar with possession I would suggest that you leave it to an exorcist, you can inadvertently cause more damage to your client. For example, dissociative identity disorder happens to a person's mind when a traumatic event such as abuse occurs. Possession and exorcism is actually considered by most exorcists to be a traumatic event. If the possession is not handled carefully the victim's mind will dissociate producing another personality. The mind's ability to produce alternate personalities by dissociating has been known to be an infinite number.

How to tell if someone is possessed

A question that is asked of me a lot is how I can tell between a dissociative (alternate personality) and a demon. I tell people that it isn't very hard if you know what death looks like. The fulfilling function that a demon drives a person to is death. As the body decays the skin on the face tightens causing the eyes to widen, the lips to reveal the teeth and the tongue begins to swell out of the mouth. This is the face of a demon and he image of Satan. Man is created in the image of God but in death man receives the image of Satan through sin. Anytime you are talking with a person and this event happens for long periods of time it is possible a demon is looking can at you.

The legend of gorgons originates from the ancient Greeks who would watch as bodies decay. To them it was a horrific sight. When people began to touch dead bodies ancient cultures noticed that these people began to present an eerie similarity to the dead bodies. In Jewish culture it is forbidden for a Jew to touch a dead body for fear they may obtain familiar spirits (dybbuk) or the sin of the deceased. However, when another voice that did not belong to the person came forward they began to either believe that a loved one was talking to them or a god. Take a look at some of the images on the next page from the various cultures around the world. Notice how eerily similar they are. These are the faces of demons. If you study this subject matter you'll be able to understand the difference between demonic possession and DID/MPD.

128

CULT AND OCCULT MIND CONTROL

This is where your training in NLP, hypnosis, psychology, cold reading and body language come into play. I learned these areas of mind control just so that I could notice the symptoms of occult/cult mind control. Should I notice any symptoms of mind control or brain washing I will attempt the necessary means of trying to bring the person out of the control of the cult. You will notice as you obtain more cases and see a pattern of occult/cult abuse that victims of these groups will not budge in their beliefs. They will even attack your character mentally or even slander you. They have enacted the metaphysical *law of belief*, which tells us that whatever you believe with feeling and conviction becomes reality. This metaphysical knowledge in the hands of a cult leader can be dangerous. However, it is always important to show love and to never respond with hatred toward people who have been brainwashed. Should you invoke anger out of them you are only feeding the fire of occult/cult mind control.

You need to understand that these people believe they are treated as outcasts of society and the church. They believe that since they are not saved that they have no choice but to go head on into the occult world. Sometimes the source of these people getting involved in the occult is due to the church itself. The church singles out certain sins rather than looking at sin as equal and as a whole as it should do.

My point is that a liar is no different than a thief, and a thief is no different than a murderer in God's eyes. All have sinned and fall short of the glory of God (Romans 3:23). God bases his judgments upon man through The Ten Commandments. However, the Catholic Church and some other Protestant branches have taken it upon themselves to single out certain sins as more sinful than others. An example is the homosexual movement. Rather than tell the public that homosexuality is no different than an adulterer or thief in God's eyes the church has singled out the sin causing more homosexuals to either leave the church or form groups to counteract the dogma of the church. Through those movements we now have homosexual churches that accept the idea of gay/lesbian marriage which is not Bible based. Now the church is faced with a headache of sorts to appease and convict homosexuals of sin at the same time. If the Catholic Church and Protestant Church would have just accepted these people in the first place and teach them how all sin is equal in God's eyes the Christian Church would not be faced with such a problem. This is the same that happened with adulterers and fornicators who formed pornographic movements in the 60's; the same applies to occultists and cult leaders. These people were told that their sin was overwhelmingly bad and that there was a limit on forgiveness from God (which is not Biblical). Being faced with limitations the idea came to their minds that they would be faced with Hell fire. So they came up with the analogy of "Why not just jump in?" If you ever talk with a Satanist and ask them if they will either go to Heaven or Hell they will answer "Hell". What is shocking is the fact that the majority of these people I talked with use to be Catholic.

The other source that drives these people to the occult/cults is overbearing self righteous parents. Once parents discover something in their child's room that is kept in secret a self righteous parent will either shun or verbally abuse their child. If they find pornographic pictures of women or men this type of abuse may drive them to pornography and later into the sex industry. Most children who later become homosexuals become curious of the same sex at the age of thirteen. They will keep their desire to themselves until a parent discovers something about their hidden life. The parent becomes heart broken and verbally abuses their child; worse yet even physical abuse. Should a priest sexually abuse a child that type of trauma stays with them as they have tried to dissociate from the event. Though the core personality may have forgotten about the abuse another personality remembers it and feels unworthiness. The same applies to occult/cult members. Occult/cult victims seek acceptance into a group with a common trauma. Once discovering a connection with others their inner hatred for their parents and the church manifests outward as the group meets in secret. More extreme groups will meet in public places to make a statement against parental and church authority.

As occult/cult leaders obtain power and influence they will tend to keep their followers with mind control. A good tactic they will use is either drug addiction (stimulants or depressants) or drugs that will influence mind control such as alcohol to entice drunkenness, cigarettes to appear cool and sexy. More potent forms of drug use are MDMA or better known as Ecstasy which has the effect of creating a deep connection and love for people. LSD (lysergic acid diethylamide), a psychoactive drug and stimulant (along with Ecstasy), is one of the most powerful hallucinogens on the black market and occult/cult leaders will use it and have their followers see images, hear sounds and feel sensations that seem real. Again, *seeing* is *believing*, with *belief* becomes *reality* and the cult leader helps his followers to enact the metaphysical law of belief. An example of drug cult indoctrinated mind control is Charles Manson who controlled his followers with drugs. Manson also used sex addiction to control his members by allowing them to feel as if they were a part of something, a sense of importance and being loved. When Manson felt that his followers were under his control, he had a few of them perform brutal murders. Another example of using sex in the occult/cult is the Raelian movement in Quebec, Canada. The Raelian cult uses beautiful sexy women to entice outside men to sleep with them. With the men now having had sex with these women are more apt to want to join the sex cult to get more sex. Sex can be used for addictive purposes like drugs for the cult to hold onto new members.

Understanding the way hypnosis works will help you to even discover hypnotic drug abuse. There are drugs out their such as *Sodium Pentathol* and *Sodium Amitol* that are in a class that effect the functions of the central nervous system which allows a person to be more open to hypnotic suggestions.

Some satanic cults will even go as far as to abuse female followers to deliberately cause their mind to dissociate producing an alternative personality that they can control. They bring out a sexual personality in a female follower who likes to have sex and have them prostitute for money. These female followers don't remember a thing because the alternative personality that is prostituting will carry all the memories of the sexual encounters she had. Don't believe this happens? If not then you need to get out of the house and study cults more and the sick and twisted minds of cult leaders.

PRESCRIPTION DRUGS

Knowing about medical drugs and the effects they have on people can help you to make a determination over whether or not to proceed with a case. When you are interviewing your client and they inform you that they are on prescription drugs you should have a general idea of how the drug works. Most prescription drugs prescribed for mental illness in the United States are for anxiety disorders. Below are the lists of prescription drugs that are prescribed for the various abnormal behaviors. The object of these medications is to allow the patient to relax from their symptoms but can also help in the journey to the cure, depending on the medication. Keep in mind that I am not a professional on prescription drugs but rather have allowed myself to become familiar with them to better help my clients.

Haldol and **Zyprexa** are the typical first treatments prescribed for people with schizophrenia. They are known as palliatives; they do not cure the disease, they only lessen the symptoms. These medications also affect other areas of the brain which can leave very unpleasant side effects. People who experience side effects from these medications often stop taking them which can lead to negative consequences. The purpose for these medications is to block the postsynaptic receptor sites of dopamine which keeps dopamine from activating the postsynaptic neuron. You should learn how neurons work so you can understand how drugs affect the central and peripheral nervous systems.

Zyprexa is also used in the treatment of Mania and Psychotic Depression.

Lithium is also used in the treatment of Mania and is mainly a mood stabilizer.

Depakote is a mood stabilizer and is used in the treatment of Bipolar Disorder.

Prozac, Zoloft and **Paxil** are antidepressants. Prozac is used for the treatment of depression while Zoloft for panic disorder and Paxil for Obsessive-Compulsive Disorder, Bulimia and Social Phobia. These medications are known as Selective Serotonin Reuptake Inhibitors (SSRIs) which block the re-absorption of serotonin.

Benzodiazepines are antianxiety/anxiolytic medications for the treatment of Insomnia, Situational Anxiety, Generalized Anxiety Disorder and Panic Disorder. Benzodiazepines affect the central nervous system. More specifically they affect the neurotransmitter GABA which slows things down in the brain and gives the patient calmness; which causes a problem because they are also highly addictive.

Ritalin is a stimulant and is usually prescribed for ADHD.

OCCULT SYMBOLS AND RITUAL ABUSE

In my book Mechanics of Demonology I list several satanic and magick symbols but I want to make the point that symbols are everywhere. We see them in our daily lives when we go to work, play and even on vacation. Symbols have a profound effect on the public, warning us of danger, providing information or defining a corporation (A logo). However, there is a darker side to the use of symbols and in the way occult/cult groups use them for mind control.

At a young age I wanted to learn ninjitsu. I discovered that ninjas had to mediate and draw symbols in the air during their mediations. As a pastor, in part of a blessing I make the sign of the cross over a person place or thing. Cult leaders will use symbols to influence their follower's unconscious minds. The conscious mind may not be aware of it but the unconscious mind is. When we see objects, people, events, or places they can trigger a memory to come forward. Cult leaders will train their followers using symbols to place psychological *anchors* in the unconscious mind. When these cult leaders show a symbol it can unconsciously trigger an action that the cult leader is looking for. Anchors are simple ways to trigger responses out of an individual. If you want a person to feel loved whenever you are around all you need to do is be present whenever love shows up. This way a person's unconscious mind will relate you with love, so when you meet with that special someone they will feel loved. The same holds true for negative outcomes. If you do not want a person to relate you with something negative then do not be around events or situations that are negative. For example, people who gossip are known as gossipers because they are always around conversations that involve negative gossip. Sports products are not known as sports products because they are healthy; they are known as sports products because the advertisers use athletes in their commercials. Companies can produce an unhealthy product and still have it known as a sports product as long as athletes are used to promote it. This is called social psychology in which psychologists study the human behavior of people in the environment. Want to get a specific message out to the public about your product? Just ask a social psychologist. If I were to take a Scotsman who wears a kilt and place him in front of men's and women's restrooms in the United States, would he see the symbol of the ladies skirt as a sign to use that room to relieve himself? How would you think people would react if I placed two different signs on two different doors that led to the same lobby? One door said Men and the other door said Women, even though one is the entrance and the other an exit. Do you think that people would take this literally even though both doors connect to the same lobby? Surprisingly the answer is yes; this is called perceptual sets. The symbols present a sign of authority and a person's superego forces them to obey the signs. This is the same perspective that occult/cult leaders use to control their followers. You would be surprised to see what cult leaders are able to do to a normal person who appears stable. A good book to read is Sun Tzu's The Art of War. In it Sun conditions and disciplines people using fear tactics to force people to obey commands. Many cults use the same fear tactics to control their people into submission.

Ancient pictographs may hold keys to opening the knowledge of Genesis 6:1-4 and the Book of Enoch, and may open hidden knowledge to understanding demonic functions.

THE 9 FUNCTIONS OF DEMONS

Many preternatural investigators assume to know the functions and characteristics of demons. I've noticed over the years that they will research how demons function and assume that demons react tactically in certain ways. Though your research may conclude on a certain aspect of the demonic, you should know that demons are unpredictable in several fashions. There is a way to know the characteristics and functions of demons without researching them. I have compiled all nine functions of demons that are outlined in the Bible for you to save you time and energy. Knowing and understanding these functions will help you to diagnosis demonic activity right away.

1. **Enticement or Temptation (James 1:14)** - Demons will often seduce or draw people to sin and break the divine law of God. By doing this allows them to gain a grip on their victim's life leading to the next functions below. A good example is a demon may tempt a person to perform occult acts leading them to inadvertently open a door allowing a demon in their life.

2. **Deceive or Deception (1 Timothy 4:1-2)** – Demons will often deceive people by presenting a piece of truth, and helping people make bad decisions. They will lie to people to help them blow things out of proposition so they won't experience the fruits of the Holy Spirit (Peace, love, grace...). In a haunting a demon may plant deceptive ideas in the minds of a married couple to cause a separation leading to a divorce. In children they will cause them to influence their parents. In worse cases demons will mimic mental illness to deceive loved ones. The victim will claim they are possessed forcing loved ones to believe they've gone insane ultimately causing a family to isolate the family member who is victimized.

3. **Enslave (Romans 815; 2 Timothy 2:26)** – Demons will entrap people into addictive sin. Much like chaining a person down to a chair and force feeding them. Demons know the more they entrap a person to addiction they will open the door more to become their master. In a haunting a person can be seen as a puppet of a demon when fear strikes them or they fear a reaction by a demonologist or exorcist when they come to visit. Another form of enslavement in a haunting is a backlash upon a preternatural investigator who researches a haunting. They may find themselves under attack in their own home. This is usually a give away that a demon is claiming ownership or has become the master of its victims life.

4. **Torment (2 Timothy 1:7; 1 John 4:18)** – Demons cause torment in multiple ways by either possession or causing anxiety to the point that fear sets in.

5. **Compulsion & Drive (Luke 8:29)** – The old phrase "No rest for the wicked" applies here. Demons like to cause pressure upon their victims allowing them to stay up and do things late at night. They will often fill their victims with so much fear that they appear to have a mental disorder such as Obsessive Compulsive Disorder (OCD). In a haunting as soon as attacks set in, parents may find themselves overly watching their children, continuously making sure things are in working order in their home, making sure sharp objects are put away. The victim appears to be reacting the same way as a subject would to appease a wicked king.

6. **Defile (Titus 1:15)** – Demons can defile people in several ways, whether by stealing their innocence from sin to physical attacks such as raping a woman. They will cause disgusting images to appear in a victims mind while they pray to remove all images that allow a person to focus on Christ. Demons will make people addicted to things to cause self-defilement such as pornography, and distorting their spiritual life by forcing them into the worship of a false religion.

7. **Teach (1 Timothy 4:1)** – Demons will teach people false doctrines to allow for their victims to feel that their attacks they receive are justified toward them. Other forms of teaching are the spreading of new theologies whether it is personal or the start of a new religion. As an exorcist this is the hardest thing to get through during the start of deliverance counseling. A demonized person will often be lead by a demon to believe in a false doctrine to place up a wall of intellect. The best way to get through the intellect of a person is to not even go there at all. Rather, use the divine law of God to cut through the intellect by using a person's conscience. Often simply using the perfect law of God itself will cause a demon to come forward. When you have to interview your client or counsel them and their own personal theology that isn't biblical comes to the surface use the law and go around the intellect. Should a demon confront you through them start interrogating it on how it got in the person. If it lies, which it will, ask the holy Spirit in Jesus name to cause the demon torment until it tells the truth.

8. **Cause Illness (Luke 13:11)** – Not every illness is caused by a demon but demons will cause symptoms that appear similar to psychological and physical weakness. I say weakness because the person may feel fine and may mention that they feel weak.

Their spirit is driven which is a good sign that something demonic is causing the illness. The flesh is weak but the spirit is willing.

9. **Produce Restlessness** – Demons produce tactics that can remove personal harmony, peace of mind, physical well-being and fellowships with others.

HOW TO CONDUCT RESEARCH

To often newer demonologists go about investigating a claim and make to many assumptions that hurt people rather than solve the problem. Worse yet is coming up with new ideas that cause arguments among other demonologists. The main problem is a few demonologists will tend to make a claims and stating their findings are fact. This upsets other demonologists who stand on other principles that show their findings to be counteractive. Either someone is lying to make themselves look good or someone has to be telling the truth.

How then can the preternatural community overcome this painful dilemma?

There is a need for research in demonology to find constructive knowledge to help humanity counter act the demonic threat. Since most churches like to use people with psychology background it is best for a demonologist to understand how to do research. By conducting proper scientific research not only will the preternatural community remove false findings but demonologists will stop getting at each others throats. Demonologists can stop basing their methods of investigating demons from old school ideas, and continue on basing their findings from proven scientific research.

Many believe that scientific research involves the investigation but what you are actually doing is a study. True scientific research involves 1) A theory or hunch, 2) a hypothesis, 3) predictions, with operational definitions, 4) and evidence. You must first come up with a *theory* or *hunch* of a certain subject matter. You must then come up with a *hypothesis* that will predict what will happen, and then identify *predict* what will happen in your study proving your hypothesis. After the study you collect data and review your findings. Should your findings or data not support your hypothesis then you must go back and review your hypothesis statement, make a new one and perform a new study. This may sound like a lot of work but it actually isn't. Here is a sample of scientific research.

A teenager name Ann *theorizes* that her mother is lame and won't let her go out with her boyfriend out on a date. Her *hypothesis* is that when she asks her mother she will say no and bash her boyfriend verbally. Ann then performs a *study* and asks her mother if she can go out with her boyfriend on a date. During her *study* Ann discovers that her *hypothesis* was wrong and that in fact mom is cool and was excited when Ann asked her. Ann's mom even went as far as to say positive things about Ann's boyfriend. Ann must now go back *review* the *data* and make a *new hypothesis*.

The thing about scientific research is that it cannot be private but rather be displayed or published among colleagues. This way the research becomes a *testable theory* allowing other researchers to perform the same research using the *same data and hypothesis*. This way even if another demonologist wanted to refute your theory he/she may inadvertently prove your theory. When colleagues test your research and the data comes out accurate 95% of the time then your research is proven.

For other demonologists to test your theories you can publish your work or simply ask a colleague to perform the same research the way you did. There are a lot of self-publishing websites out there that you can publish your research at. Sadly there isn't any Demonology Association of any kind like the American Psychological Association that you can take your research to and have it tested. You simply will have to publish your work and get the word out to other demonologists.

So how can this method of scientific research work for demonology? In a nutshell it can remove suggestions, ideas, false findings, assumptions and test the current ideas that are commonly accepted to find facts. An example is the idea that burning a Ouija board will release a spirit. This is commonly accepted, however the church for centuries has been telling people to burn items of divination to cast out the spirit and release a person from the bonds of Satan. This is commonly accepted in the church today due to Acts (19:18-20) when a group of witches accepted Christ and gathered all their spell casting material and items of divination and burned them. The idea that people shouldn't burn a Ouija board for fear of releasing the spirit upon the victim because it lost its item of attachment doesn't hold ground. There simply is not enough evidence to prove this theory. I myself have conducted research into this theory and haven't found anything that proves it. There is evidence by the church that reveals that if a person renounces the use of the Ouija board, and then burns it the spirit is cast out from presents of the person when they come to Christ.

By each demonologist taking the time to properly conduct scientific research and test each others research we can have a more productive and united demonology community.

Types of Studies

When you come up with a theory, make a hypothesis you must then proceed with a study. Below are the types of studies you can use to collect data.

Case Studies – Detailed descriptions an individual being studied. There are usually different types of case studies that involve the same criteria. You may want to do research on possession cases and review possession cases from past studies to find material that supports your theory.

Observational Studies – This type of study is what it says. You may want to conduct research into the behavior of demons from the possessed by only observing exorcisms and writing down your findings on what you have observed. The object of this type of study is to not get involved and to only observe. You could say this type of study is conducting *field research*.

Psychological Tests – Media that is used in evaluating emotions and personality traits such as interests, emotional states, aptitudes, abilities and values. How can a test help in the study of demonology? Any interesting research study may be to test the behavior of a possessed person before and after an exorcism. Would there be a difference in personality?

Any test that you provide a person or group must be valid and reliable and have standardized procedures of scoring.

Surveys – Surveys are direct questionnaires that ask people specific questions about experiences, attitudes and opinions. Though not as reliable as tests, surveys do have there value in discovering which areas to begin research. Keep in mind that you must remove all bias when creating a survey.

Correlational Studies – This is a descriptive study that looks for a relationship between two criteria. A *positive correlation* is when two criteria have an increasing high value over the course of the study. Their relationship appears to be the same and match on a graph. Such as there is a positive correlation between Christian holidays and the increase of demonic activity. In a positive correlation two criteria appear to be moving up and down in an even or similar flow. A *negative correlation* is where two criteria appear to have no relationship at all. The high values of one criterion do not match the low values of another. When one criterion is not similar to another over the course of a study then there is no positive correlation. However, this does not mean that two values have no correlation it just means that one is negatively effecting another. You may notice in your research that as one value rises the other values lowers in a repeated pattern each time you conduct a study.

Experiment – This is a controlled test of your hypothesis in which you manipulate one variable to see if it affects another. In conducting an experiment you will be manipulating the *independent variable* to see how it will affect the *dependant variable*. You may want to conduct an experiment to see if Ouija board usage (independent variable) has an effect on people going to church (dependant variable). In doing experiments keep in mind that there are *control groups* and *experimental groups*. Each receives the same treatment in some fashion. However, the control group is the group that you have access to with a *placebo*, while the experimental group is the group that you *manipulate* with the independent variable.

There are *single blind studies*, in which the participates don't know if they are a part of either the control group or the experiment group, or *double-blind studies* in which the people running the experiment don't know which people are in which group. The object of the experimenter is to not give any hints to people of which group they belong too.

TYPES OF RESEARCH FIELDS

At one point I was asked a question from a person wanting to know if there were different types of demonology fields. I responded that I wasn't sure but after review I identified several fields of potential research that is currently being done by demonologists. Whether demonologists know they are performing them or not is the question. Below are the identified fields of demonology research with their definitions.

Experimental Demonology – Conducting experiments that tests theories in a laboratory environment that allows the demonologist to gather data. An experimental demonologist may only wish to observe exorcisms or create his own study in a controlled environment.

Archeological Demonology – The study of conducting archeological research to investigate demonic claims and how the terrestrial environment reacts to demonic beings.

Religious/Christian Demonology – The study and research of preternatural investigators who work or operate with a Christian Church to investigate demonic claims. Generally these type of demonologists are trusted by the church to gather empirical evidence to sanction a sacerdotal service.

Occult Demonology – The use of occult methods or the study of the occult in relation to demons. Generally people who study this form of demonology are *occultists* or in a more positive light *occult specialists* who attempt to remove occult media and rites.

Biological Demonology – The study of how plants and animals react prior, during and after a demonic haunting. Research can be conducted down to a cellular level to understand how demons can have an effect on the physical structures of life.

Investigative Demonology – The study or research of obtaining evidence to support the existence of supernatural entities by the use of equipment that is sensitive to demons. Investigative demonologists may test different pieces of equipment on investigations to understand what media gather data better.

CONCLUSION

I hope the knowledge in this book was beneficial to you in your search to become a demonologist. There is a lot to know to become one that is important to the welfare of your clients. My last bit of advice to you, and most important of all, is to get to know your client. Even though you are not a professional such as a medical doctor or in the health service, treat yourself as if you were a professional just as you would in running a business. When faced with a situation ask yourself, what would a medical physician or psychologist do? Or what would a policeman do? I say this because you may find yourself being faced with these situations or helping these professionals. Would you be angry if you were a medical doctor and some amateur told your patient to get off meds? Would you be angry if you were an exorcist and some amateur told your client that they weren't possessed? This type of thinking under minds and disrespects the knowledge of these professionals. As an exorcist I can tell you that I get upset when some amateurs move in on a case I am working on without my permission. I especially get angry when they decide to burn sage in an attempt to cast out a demon. All the months or years of hard work, counseling and deliverance sessions can all be undone by a single know it all. I've had my share of know it alls and I must say they do not impress me. I have a mental policy when it comes down to working with new individuals in the field of deliverance ministry. If they screw up and act like they know something when they don't, I never work with them again. Why? Because I care for my clients and the last thing I want is for someone to get hurt.

What really upsets me are know it alls who have not a clue in the preternatural and bash others to make themselves look good. They'll bash respected demonologists and exorcists in the field who have proven talent and perfected their craft. There are also the types of know it alls who have been in college and taken a few psychology classes and try to interpret theology. If you are one of these people please leave theology to the religious leaders and apply your college major to a specific need in the paranormal; you will be more valuable to the community of demonologists this way.

As you can see from the curriculum in this book there is a lot to learn. I would advise that you develop a study in your home and obtain books on the subjects outlined in the curriculum. Many make the mistake of purchasing books directed in demonology rather than the studies that are needed to be a successful a demonologist. If you only study demons but happen to fall on a case with weird biological objects how would you handle the case? Understanding some biology will help you to know the specifics of how something biological came about in the case. These studies in the curriculum will also help you to develop relationships with professional individuals who can assist with scientific questions. I personally know a physicist who works for the U.S. Government along with exorcists, ekballists, demonologists, pastors, a criminal profiler, occult specialists, psychologists, and people with medical training to assist in deliverance.

By now you've read this entire book, reading these last words of advice and guidance. Now that you have come to the end learn as much as you can and be humble and learn from much older and experienced demonologists. However, my last bit of advice is to stay true to God's word (Holy Bible) and don't backslide. I know that it is hard but you must. You will be tempted and enticed to do things you don't want to do. *Resist.* You will feel depressed at times. *Resist.* You will feel at times as though the whole world is coming down on you. *Resist.* There will be times when you feel your faith shaken. *Get back up.* Others will be your critics and judge you. *Love on them.* When you face the intelligence of a demon from the possessed a demon will remind you of your past sins, when he does *remind him of his future* (Revelation 20:10). And no matter how hard it can be try your best to keep *The 10 Commandments* (Exodus 20).

Whether you have the makings to be a demonologist or not it takes time and skill to gain experience as long as you want it. Experience doesn't happen over night so you must be patient and take the time to know your enemy. With faith, works of obedience, initiative and the teachings of Jesus Christ you will be on the path to become a great demonologist.

ABOUT THE AUTHOR

G.P. Haggart is a theologian in Central Michigan. He holds a bachelors of theology and teaches Christian theology, apologetics and deliverance and had been an affiliate of the American Psychological Association. As a Christian Counselor and expert deliverance ministry G.P. Haggart has conducted over twenty exorcisms and ekballisms of advanced stages of diabolic possession, evaluated demonic cases on a psychological level, debunked cases with demonic claims, assisted criminal profilers on occult related cases involving possible possession and blessed thirty plus homes with stage 4 and 5 demonic activity. As a church and ministry planter G.P. Haggart has assisted pastors and church planters on how to stay compliant with state and federal laws to help expand church growth throughout the United States.

BIBLIOGRAPHY

Alphesus, A. (1903), Complete Hypnotism, Mesmerism, Mind-Reading and Spiritualism How to Hypnotize: Being an Exhautive and Practical System of Method, Application, and Use.

Benedict, Elsie Lincoln & Benedict, Ralph Paine (1921), How to Analyze People on Sight.

Cash, Psy.D, Adam (2002). Psychology For Dummies. Hoboken,New Jersey: Wiley Publishing, Inc.

Goll, James W. (2010). Deliverance from Darkness. Grand Rapids, Michigan: Chosen Books.

Haddock, M.Ed., M.A., L.P., Deborah Bray (2001). The Dissociative Identity Disorder Sourcebook. New York, New York: McGraw-Hill

Havelock, Ellis (1927), Studies in the Psychology of Sex, Volumes 1-5 Sexual Inversion.

Healy, A.B., M.D., Healy & Healy, B.I., Mary Tenney (1915), Pathological Lying, Accusation, and Swindling a Study in Forensic Psychology.

Holmes, Ronald M., Holmes, Stephen T. (2009). Profiling Violent Crimes: An Investigative Tool. Thousand Oaks, California: Sage Publications, Inc.

Jones, Dantalion (2006). Mind Control 101.
Lulu, Inc.

Kohler, Dr. Kaufmann (1918), Jewish Theology, Systemtically and Historically Considered. The Macmillian Company

Maxwell, John C. (1999). The 21 Indispensable Qualities of a Leader. Nashville, Tennessee: Thomas Nelson, Inc.

Münsterberg, Hugo (1914), Psychology and Social Sanity. Doubleday, Page & Company

Myerson, M.D., A. (1914), The Journal of Abnormal Psychology, Hysteria as a Weapon in Marital Conflicts. Hospital Taunton State Hospital Papers

Powers, Melvin (1961), A Practical Guide to Self-Hypnosis. Wilshire Book Company

Pyle, William Henry (1917), The Science of Human Nature, A Psychology for Beginners. Silver, Burdett & Company

Sigmund, Freud (1920), Dream Psychology, Psychoanalysis for Beginners; Authorized English Translation by M.D. Eder. The James A. McCann Company

Taylor, Eldon (2009), Mind Programming, From Persuasion and Brainwashing to Self-Help and Practical Metaphysics. Hay House, Inc.

Tedsen, Kathleen & Rydel, Beverlee (2010). Haunted Travels of Michigan, Volume II. Holt, Michigan: Thunder Bay Press.

Temes, Ph.D, Roberta (2004). The Complete Idiot's Guide to Hypnosis. New York, New York: Penguin Group

The Bathroom Readers' Institute (2006). The Extraordinary Book of Facts and Bizarre Information. Ashland, Oregon: The Bathroom Reader's Institute.

Wade, Carole & Travis Carol (2011), Psychology.
Pearson Prentice Hall

Wiley, H. Orion (1940), Christian Theology, Volumes 1-3.
Beacon Hill Press of Kansas City

OTHER BOOKS BY
GP HAGGART

Novels

Dragon Slayer: The March on Silene (Volume 1)

After the final battle in the Roman crisis, Roman commander Georgios of Cappadocia is given a legion to secure the Province of Africa for Emperor Diocletian as he heads north. Upon arriving in Africa he falls in love with the Princess Sabra and must dethrone her mad father who issues a lottery of virgins to appease a diabolical beast. Little does he know of a sinister force that has the ear of the king.

Dragon Slayer: Wrath of the Tempest (Volume 2)

While Roman forces fight in the north, her back door is wide open and is unaware of the evil growing to the south. Satrina's most powerful weapon, the tempest, sees a strategic opportunity to attack the Roman metropolis of Leptis Magna. Georgios, Quintus, Pen, Medhu, Makeda and their new friends, the twins Dozar and Celzar race against time to stop the forces of darkness and an ancient evil from leveling the city. Meanwhile, evil returns to Silene as Sabra reluctantly joins forces with the obsessed tribune Atticus to prevent her father the king from taking back power and starting a civil war. *Coming in 2015.*

Non-Fiction

Mechanics of Demonology – *"Pastor Haggart has written Mechanics of Demonology from his years of training and experience in deliverance ministry to provide this knowledge to you! While it will not make you a demonologist it will keep that blank look off your face when someone asks... How do you know?"*

-William (Bill) Vaile Founder of United Paranormal International

Protestant exorcist and pastor G.P. Haggart breaks down the study of demonology for educational purposes. Forward by Demonologist Tracy Bacon. G.P. Haggart tells the story of his first encounter with a demon that propelled him sixteen years later to battle demons and empower victims of demonic haunts. Discover the knowledge needed to confront demons, how to investigate a demonic haunt, how to debunk a demonic haunt, characteristics of demons, the science of possession, the origin and nature of evil, the four theories of the origins of demons, exorcism, diabolical metaphysics and much more.

Mechanics of Demonology, Volume 2: The Intermediate Level - *Some imagery not meant for younger readers.* The upgrade to Mechanics of Demonology is here! Christian Theologian G.P. Haggart dives deeper into the occult realm and reveals what is hidden in the shadows. In Mechanics of Demonology, Volume 2: The Intermediate Level, you'll learn intermediate knowledge of demonology that will help you to battle demons and identify occult interaction. Learn Demonic Psychology and know what a demon is thinking, Intermediate Occultology and see what is hidden in our world, Introduction to the Preternatural to grasp the knowledge of demons in the past, Anatomy of Demonic Possession to know how possession starts and how it is cast out and much more!

Just $29.95 on paperback!

The Ekballist - *Based on true stories.* The Ekballist is a narrative account of one man's life encounters and battles with the forces of evil. After living a life as an atheist and later an occultist, he becomes possessed by an evil force. Not wishing for anyone else to experience the evil he witnessed, he obtains hidden knowledge that helps others to overcome Satan and his demons.

Just $9.95 on paperback, and $1.99 on Kindle!

Screech Owl: The Lie Behind Lilith – In August of 2009 exorcist G.P. Haggart encounters a possessed woman in Clare, Michigan whose demon describes the demonics mysterious origins.

G.P. Haggart, author of the popular textbook on demons, *Mechanics of Demonology*, brings together the manuscripts and legends of one of history's most diabolical demons. In Screech Owl, G.P. Haggart exposes the lie that demons would lead you to believe. You will be shocked to discover the truth behind the legendary demon queen known as Lilith.

Just $0.99 on Kindle!

The God Who is Still Here - Did Jesus exist? Is there evidence for the historical Jesus? Do you have trouble finding Jesus? Are you struggling with atheism, agnosticism or backsliding cause you have questions? The God Who is Still Here, is a booklet by theologian G.P. Haggart that will help you through the tough questions; help you find the answers you seek to find Jesus and to know that God is still here.

Just $0.99 on Kindle!

Financial

Let Them Eat Cash: Why the Middle Class Does Not Get Rich - Ever wonder why you're not rich or financially secure? In, Let Them Eat Cash, you'll find out what you're doing wrong and find out how to fix. Learn what the Middle Class is doing wrong, what the rich think about it, what the rich do differently, and techniques which will help you start you on a path to becoming financially secure!

Just $2.99 on Kindle!

**How to make Extra Money: 18 Guaranteed Tip$ to put more money in your pocket$!** - Need extra money but don't know where to start? Tired of losing money to expenses and liabilities and have no money to save? Tired of get rich quick scams that take your money? Learn 18 guaranteed tip$ that will put more money in your pockets!

Just $1.99 on Kindle!

Go to **www.ekballist.com** for more information on books by

GP Haggart

29968500R00093

Made in the USA
Middletown, DE
08 March 2016